Social Justice Autobiographies

Inequality, Injustice & America's Incarcerated

Print book: 978-1-962385-07-7
E-book: 978-1-962385-08-4

Zo Media Productions, LLC
P.O. BOX 862
BRISTOW OK 74010

All money raised from sales
goes toward sustaining
the

Forward

Megan McDrew

"Adverse childhood experiences are the
single greatest unaddressed public health
threat facing our nation today."
-- Robert Block, former president of the
American Academy of Pediatrics

In a world where fairness falters and our criminal
punishment system equates to massive inequalities,
cruel punishments and incredible suffering, this book
stands as a beacon of courage, truth and justice. All of
this evolved through incredible collaborations between
myself, a select number of my sociology students at
UCSC and Ivan Kilgore, founder and director of the
United Black Family Scholarship Foundation who is
currently serving a Life Without Parole sentence in
California.

As a sociology instructor at UCSC, I taught social
justice at least once an academic year. I also instructed
sociology through Hartnell College at the Correctional
Training Facility (CTF) of Soledad prison, assisting the
incarcerated residents the opportunity to receive an
AA Degree while behind bars. An assignment I offered
my campus-based students was the opportunity to
write their "social justice autobiographies", asking the
students to reflect on one or more factors that influenced
their understanding and experience of social justice, or
lack thereof. Ivan Kilgore was also a student of mine

at Salinas Valley Prison in my sociology course around that same time, spring 2021. He was, and still is, quite dedicated to writing and empowering fellow prisoners to write their stories. Putting our various strengths and ideas together, we decided to offer all incarcerated folks across our nation to take part in an essay writing contest using the same social justice prompt I offered to UCSC students. After receiving hundreds of essays, and having select UCSC student volunteers type and edit them, the project was taken on by doctoral students at Stony Brook University where they chose 24 of the more powerful essays and composed them into the book you now have in your hands.

Through teaching sociology, a subject that challenges us to think deeply about the impacts of race, gender, sexuality, and class in our daily lives, stories unfold that give testament to the trauma, neglect, inequalities, marginalization and adversity faced by the authors prior to entry into the system of incarceration. Many come from familial abuse and instability, gangs, poverty, homelessness, addiction, and entrenched violence. Some, but not most, come from wealth, mansions in Pebble Beach, military and police backgrounds, even engineers with doctorates. I spend one or two days a week with men who have murdered someone through gang or domestic violence, who have raped, molested, kidnapped, and tortured. People who have robbed, assaulted, dealt drugs, were addicted to drugs, on and on. Over my 10 years of going inside prisons and jails, I've instructed men of all different criminal backgrounds who are set on the path of transformation through higher education, a most treasured opportunity in prison. As a sociologist with a passion for radical compassion and equal justice, I've read hundreds of sociological autobiographies, leading to the proceeding conclusions.

When you go into a prison or jail, you will see that there are a wide range of reasons people are there that can be summed in one or two words – murder, gang involvement, rape, second degree manslaughter, etc. Behind those criminal sentences is a complex tapestry of social and environmental conditions coupled with poor decisions that led up to the point of incarceration, subsequently doing hard time in a state or federal prison. Behind subsequent criminal sentences lies a tapestry of societal conditions, often trapping the most vulnerable in a punitive web. In this disorienting space of captivity, isolation and mundanity, there is little to no room for growth while the familial and societal reasons why people end up in cages remain unaddressed.

Mumia Abu-Jamal, now imprisoned for 44 years, says, "ignorance is the root of all crime." Ignorance is also at the at the root of mass incarceration. If we, as a society, understood the complexities of the lives before incarceration, could get closer to the men, women and children in detention, and see how harmful prisons are in the US, we would be one step closer to prison abolition through compassion and knowledge. We would also see hearts and minds very much like our own, yearning for connection, authentic relationships and healing.

Upon entering most any prison or jail, we would also see these institutions filled with people of color, a reminder that prisons are nothing more than modern day plantations where the state is the master and prisoners are the slaves, enduring a slow social death, stripped of all rights or abilities to be anything but the one thing the system designed them to be – a property of the state, a prisoner, a criminal. It is our own ignorance and apathy about the systems and institutions that run our lives that have created mass incarceration, unknowingly caging the most powerless, uneducated and traumatized among us.

Take your time with these brutally honest stories, revealing that the majority of people who end up in prison come from deeply traumatic, abusive and neglectful pasts. That, if given the right amount of support, attention, mentorship, and yes, love, they would have had the opportunities like the physically free among us. Yet, they slipped through the cracks, ignored and deplored individuals now living in captivity, deeply isolated, suffering in silence, yearning to be understood and to ultimately give back to the communities in which they hurt.

It is a common saying that hurt people hurt people and healed people heal people. As you immerse yourself in these personal, raw accounts of familial and social injustices that affect people of color and those living in poverty at statistically much higher rates, I ask that you bear witness to the resilience, introspection, and evolution of individuals navigating a system that often overshadows their humanity and possibility of positive transformation. Each story serves as a testament to the transformative power of empathy and the urgent need for a more compassionate approach to justice. These autobiographies illuminate the shadows of the prison walls , urging us to all rethink, reform, and most importantly, empathize.

By and large, prisoners are living invisible and fear, in contaminated filth and disgrace while the rest of the country believes our safety rests on the unfreedom of others. I will tell you one final thing and it is this: our safety and security rests in fixing the many broken institutions in this country, beginning with the family but also schools, the church, military, the government, and last but certainly not least, the prison industrial complex and mass incarceration. Releasing the millions of people who are caged in this country will not harm you or your children, especially if we insist that prisoners are treated with dignity and a direct focus on rehabilitation, restorative justice, equity and accountability.

May these narratives serve as a catalyst for dialogue, reflection and ultimately, transformative action. The power to reshape the narrative of incarceration lies within each of us. Let us carry the torch of empathy forward, breaking the chains of indifference, and striving for a society where redemption, healing, and real justice prevail.

> "You are not a victim for sharing your story. You are a survivor setting the world on fire with your truth. And you enver know who needs your light, your wamrth, and raging courage." -- Alex Elle

Megan McDrew founded and directs The Transformative Justice Center of Monterey County which houses a rehabilitation program offered in prison, Exercises in Empathy. Megan brings 25-30 people from the community into prison weekly to dialogue with the incarcerated residents at CTF Soledad prison, building bridges of humanity, insight and healing between the incarcerated and the public. For 7 years, she served as faculty member in the UC system with UC Santa Cruz and UC Merced as well as an instructor at Hartnell Community College and 2 prisons in South Monterey County, committed to helping the incarcerated obtain AA degrees. She also works for the public defender's office in Santa Cruz assisting with juvenile Franklin hearing statements. Last but not least, Megan is a freelance journalist for SPAN, a State Department funded e-zine based in New Delhi that focuses on Indian American education issues.

Taurus DeVault

The Prisonaire

I have been incarcerated going on ten years, wrongly convicted. I'll be winning my case soon, in which I'll be exposing the corruption of the prosecutors and others. I was a very well-known drug supplier who lived a lavish lifestyle.

Today, I am a thirty-three-year-old African American man. I was raised in a very strict household and grew up in business; my mother and father owned a grocery store, which we still have after thirty years. But the problem was that the store was in the Hood, where I saw drug dealers, money, fancy cars, women, and more all my life. Us as people, especially Black kids, growing up in the Hood we tend to learn by watching, not by formal education. So even when you have your parents tell you "Stay in school, don't drink, don't sell drugs," it's not going to work unless you move us away from the environment.

See, the problem in society is this: A lot of us don't know who we really are.

And if you don't know who you are then you will let people decide it for you. We begin to live this life of illusion and make it our reality. We think selling drugs, robbing, gangbanging and so on is *the* lifestyle just because we are around it. But it's not. We somehow told ourselves this is correct. There's a lot of people who made great choices that came from poverty. I tell people all the time, "Don't become a victim of your circumstances or situations." That's the number one thing we fail at.

I know that what everyone wants in life is an opportunity, and opportunity will cause less violence no matter where you come from. The problem is that the youth don't realize that there is opportunity in their faces, but their lifestyle and social aspects make them miss it. We need leaders out there, but nowadays the people that kids look up to are the wrong role models. You got guys and women at the age of forty doing the same thing the youth is doing.

I came up with the name "The Prisonaire" and here is my meaning behind it: Someone who truly understands they're in control of their destiny. It took me coming to prison to really, really realize that. But not only just realize it, but to take action. Listen, everyone, it's not really about "a black/white thing," but we let the things we are facing separate us. We must realize every culture lives differently, then you must realize that just because their skin is like yours doesn't mean they all think like you. Some blacks live in a suburb around whites all their life so they tend to "act white," if that's what you call it. Vice versa.

From studying psychology, practicing Islam, reading books, running businesses, and becoming a motivational speaker, I earned the Doctor title. I have helped professors, college students, business owners, and black and white people struggling, all while in prison through the mail, visits, and the telephone. I came to prison and turned my life around. I took advantage of what prison had to offer.

I want to leave everyone with a little message that is so important: the most important part of the body is the <u>HEART</u>.

For one, if the heart is spoiled the whole body becomes spoiled. But once the heart becomes pure and loving, then the whole body becomes pure. See, until we change the way we think, our actions will stay the same. Why? Because each and every one of us is the way we think, and with a new way of thinking we can find honorable ways to satisfy our desires and learn the transformation that is necessary to be successful in the social aspect of our struggle. Always remember that there is a wrong way, a right way, and a correct way to do things in life. I can guarantee you that if you do things the <u>correct way</u> in life, meaning following the rules, learning the system, and standing up for justice even if it be against yourself, I can promise you a happy life. But the problem is that a lot of us don't know how and strive to learn how to accomplish these things. Yes, I have a method to teach people. God has given me a gift.

I know I did wrong in my past. I know I destroyed my community. I feel ashamed, but I was ignorant then; and now I am going back to help make a difference in people's lives the correct way. I am an example of a reformed man who came to prison, became successful in prison, and didn't let my circumstances or situation make me a victim, and so can you.

Javar Hollins
PEACE

My grandfather told me that things were different, that things were better. He told me this when I was in the second grade. I'd come home from school after learning about the Jim Crow laws of the South, which had been done away with well before I was born.

You see, my grandfather, Robert Brent, was born in Mississippi in 1919. The story goes that he was still a child when his father ran afoul of some local white men and was forced to flee north to Michigan with his whole family. In his early years, my grandfather experienced the segregated South, the terror of open racism, northern ghettos, poverty, and the police oppression of Blacks. As a young man, he joined the military when it was still segregated and African Americans were treated as third-rate citizens. He lived through the sit-ins and marches, the dogs, the fire hoses, and the assassinations of Malcolm, Martin, and Medgar.

By the time I was in second grade, in 1987, my grandfather had reached a level of comfort and illusory freedom that his generation once feared would never come. Looking at my life through the lens of his personal history, it was clear to me that all he saw were roses. Without question, things had improved; but true social equality was still an ephemeral, distant dream. This truth was attested to when my parents fell victim to the crack epidemic. Millions had been affected by it. The crack epidemic was engineered by our own government–a government that was all too eager to sacrifice the Black community in order to fund an illegal war for the furtherance of a global power grab.

When I was 9, my class went on a field trip to an amusement park called Indiana Beach. As our buses were turning into the parking lot, several other buses filled with white kids were passing by. As they passed, the white students screamed out of their windows, calling us the N-word and whatever other racial epithets they could conjure up. My young mind couldn't comprehend how they could display such hatred and dislike for people they didn't know and who had caused them no harm.

At the age of 10, my older brother and I were placed in a home where our foster mother was white. She treated us well, but my brother had to share a bedroom with her 17-year-old son who had a Confederate flag hanging on the wall and made a habit of telling us about our "n***** lips" and "n***** noses" until we decided to do something about it. When we reacted, we were the ones who were deemed the problem.

I was 11 years old the first time I was slammed on the hood of a police car before even being asked my name, simply because I "fit the description". At age 18, I lost my life to the prison industrial complex. Not because I killed anyone, but because, according to the state of Illinois, I'm accountable for the conduct of others even though evidence showed that I had tried to stop the incident.

This is where social inequality exists between Blacks and whites in my lifetime. There are health disparities, a tech gap, wage disparities and differing sentences for the same or less severe crimes. There is a high rate of wrongful convictions, and Blacks are arrested at a much higher rate. Communities are over-policed while our schools remain underfunded and classrooms over-populated. Black unemployment is consistently higher than the national average. There are injustices towards Black people: the

Central Park Five, Rodney King, Amadou Diallo, Trayvon Martin, Tamir Rice, Laquan McDonald, Michael Brown, George Floyd, and Breonna Taylor, just to name a few.

Things are different. The blatant bigotry and systemic racism of my grandfather's era has given way to a latent and more insidious strain. I would argue that this new strain is more harmful because hidden things are easier to ignore. For far too long, we have mistakenly believed that it is social equality, or the lack thereof, that is a minority problem, but it's not. It is, however, a problem for minorities. But social inequality is an American problem.

Still, I believe that there is a path to true social justice and equality. The power rests with the people! All of the people: white, Black, brown, Native, American, Asian, Arab, immigrant, Christian, Jewish, Muslim, straight, LGBTQ+, women, and men. All of us who desire equality must fight one another's battles. The heterosexual Black man must attack homophobia with the same fervor that he resists racism. The white male executive must demand equal pay for his female counterpart. Christians Jews, and Muslims must link arms in a Godly brotherhood.

The white suburban mother must be vocally outraged over the murder of Breonna Taylor as if she was her own daughter or sister, and so on and so forth.

P.E.A.C.E.!

(Please Exercise Acceptance and Compassion Everywhere!)

Merrick Moore

A Lie is Easier to Find

When presented with an opportunity to expand on a topic such as social justice, "deep reflection" becomes a necessary tool; the portal transporting you through the wilderness of history, emotions, and tightly clutched beliefs. Anytime a group of society's people suffer injustice, especially of an unbalanced portion, there is injustice.

The opposite of social justice is injustice. This is my personal experience with social injustice. As I sat in a room watching music videos at a friend's house with his newborn, West Covina Police entered the residence. Upon exiting from the room, I was accosted and racially profiled. I was asked if I was on parole or probation, to which I curiously inquired, "Why?" I was informed they were investigating a kidnapping. I stated "I'm on parole!" I had no idea that these words would end up being the last I spoke as a free man.

As soon as I was told I was detained, I invoked my constitutional right to counsel. I was maced, punched, and assaulted, having my clothes and shoes removed. A tainted photo was taken where I'm holding my head down, then submitted to a 6 pack line-up. My shoes were taken from me and given to a detective on my case. The detective took my shoes to the crime scene where one print was found. I received no court or medical attention. Then, while in custody awaiting pretrial, the LA County Sheriff was observed by a detective, and my counsel, coaching the victim/witness on which person in the line-up to identify. Not one time did my trial attorney call either the opposing attorney, or the sheriff to address the misconduct of counsel. It was then that I transitioned to representing myself pro-der and the court had me fill out some forms.

I left the box unchecked that read "Have you received documents needed to proceed to trial?" I checked no to express that my fundamental constitutional rights were violated. The attorney was given an extension of time, despite the judge saying he would appoint another attorney (which he didn't). These events are all true. Twenty-five years later the system refuses to correct this injustice.

Now, there's no dispute that the City of West Covina Police Department detectives "conspired" illegally and falsely connected me to a crime that doesn't exist, I was charged with carjacking a minor and in the commission of the aforesaid crime committed a kidnapping. Under the state of California vehicle codes and statutes   a minor cannot be carjacked , yet, here I sit. The injustice of a false conviction steals your life, memories, birthdays, love, experiences, etc. but it also creates a hunger inside of you to voice your concerns towards all injustice. The observation and study of this injustice for long periods of time gives you a more keen perspective about the system.

Social justice would be giving me back my freedom and correcting the wrongs that have been done. I would like to make a movie one day about my experience, make music, and speak at events. It's a complete reconstruction of the individual. When you're convicted for a crime you're not guilty of , and forced to live each day shouting your innocence to whoever will listen, rlt ruins your dreams, goals, and ambitions. It does great damage to the soul.

That cosmic shift is social injustice. Our actions and decisions affect not just us but those closest to us. If I'm in a relationship with a woman who goes to work where the conditions are socially unacceptable, and each night she informs me of more women being subjected to the same conditions, what are our options? Each time she and others complain, the more retaliation ensues. Social injustice is the fear of doing the right thing and being punished or ostracized by individuals with their own agenda.

I truly believe that if more people based their decisions purely on what's right is right, and what's wrong is wrong, then social injustice would be less.

Why is it that people spend some of their time avoiding truth?

Because a lie is easier to find.

James Jones

Social Justin From Within

**Until the great mass of the people shall
be filled with a sense of responsibility for
each other's welfare, social justice can
never be attained.
--Helen Keller**

My commitment name is James Jones/CK8648, aka Sundiata Chaka Pollard, my mother's given name to her son.

My introduction to social justice, according to Delores Rene DeWitt, aka Sista' DiDi, my mother, came on July 2, 1997. Let me share:

"Gwen came by last Sunday. Isn't it something, that Gwen and I live in Northridge (kinda where it all started) and that God had already blessed us! It's true—the first school that you ever went to was California State University, Northridge. My goodness, your introduction into the world of how it is going to be.

"At that time, it was a struggle to attain higher learning in a world where that is obviously a threatening proposition to many. It is a known fact, combined with our natural gifts and talents that God creates in us, together with wisdom and knowledge, that there isn't anything they cannot conquer. Especially with one mind and one heart.

"We were detoured, distracted but determined to make it. Well, anyway, to make something, whatever that has turned out to be for each of us—the first twenty-eight students of African descent who attended the university."

My mother was a product of the Civil Rights Movement. Her mother, who was an elementary school dropout, homeschooled my mother and her three younger sisters and later acquired her GED while I was attending school. They were involved in activism through our church, their schools, and community. Delores visited South Africa on several occasions during Apartheid, returning as "DiDi" (Elder Sister). And between all of that, was the youngest at that time to graduate magna cum laude and valedictorian from UCLA.

The opposite of my mother, I was the first to serve a state sentence of life without the possibility of parole, followed by numbers. As of June 2021, I have spent twenty-eight years within the Pennsylvania's Department of Corrections.

Growing up in Pacoima (LA County) and in Philadelphia, social justice was very different. As a child in elementary school, I do not recall social justice. We sang "Lift Every Voice" and studied Martin Luther King's "I Have A Dream" speech. Back then, we had under ten TV channels. I learned a lot about the USA, current affairs, and the World, while nothing about local news in other communities.

Public school, for me, changed when I was bused to Arlington Heights Elementary in Los Angeles. Public schools for those like me had few resources—for instance, we had a harpsichord to be played by thirty-two-plus students. The other school had their own music class, in its own room, and assigned each child their own instrument. I was given a kitchen job, and I was fired. I got to build and shoot off a rocket. Mine went the farthest, five city blocks. Chasing after it, which I will never forget, internally I discriminately learned something of 'social' & 'justice' that day, about me and my environment. The school was beautiful and immaculate. Its all-white staff, students, walls, and clean rooms were a drastic change from my learning environment. That's where I chased my rocket. As I returned home, three blocks out, I sensed the hood. Five blocks out, I smelled, heard, and felt the darkened heaviness of the ghetto. I ran back faster to return than I did for my rocket. I don't know why.

Growing up in Pacoima, around my mother and father's friends and sometimes around the dinner table,I heard talk of social justice. While in Philly, I caught small talk of social justice, I think, either in 'passing the bottle' circles or from white college students teaching black children about Egypt. Saying things like its not a part of Africa! It's in the Middle East?? Even as they were planning next to "help" the Black struggle.

Under Benjamin and Katherine Crouch (Andre's parents) and family, we went down to LA to have Mayor Tom Bradley's back.   Because of my church, community, and The Boys Club, my family kept me out of school until California recognized Dr. MLK Jr's birthday as a state holiday. Later, on my own, I registered to vote for Jesse Jackson, encouraging others my age from Germantown (Philly) to do the same. If I wanted to advocate doing something for/towards social justice, I don't know.

Throughout my incarceration, now with more than ten news stations, I hear a lot about 'social justice' and every time its brought up it's in the wake of death—James Byrd, Oscar Grant, Sandra Bland, Atatiana Jefferson, Breonna Taylor, Bettie Jones, Tamir Rice, etc. etc. They all complied and died, then were charged with stacked felonious crimes.

In truth, one of the above were killed for economic justice, political justice, class, gender, sexual orientation, religion, social, civil rights or committing a felony.   Instead, each of them were murdered simply for the color of their skin. While those who murdered them received immunity and their actions were called socially justified—it was actually social injustice for those who look like me.

2021, on the *View* (6/18/21- ABC), Rep. James Clayburn (D-SC), was questioned by the panel of hosts on HR4 being blocked from covering all fifty states. Why is there compromised voting rights and voter suppression- The Civil Rights Movement ensured these rights to you and me, right?!?

My mother was attacked violently for fighting/standing up for social justice. Her mother's community was attacked for meetings and whisperings of social justice. While her siblings and ancestors were attacked for daring to dream to have even a notion of social equality and justice.

From those experiences and stories, I'm not sure what social justice actually is in full democratic practice. From that point of view, I do not believe I have been extended such privilege from the great mass of the people who say they believe in social justice

However, if you really want to know—well, pay attention! I am a Muslim. Growing up and raised in the Church- I witnessed many GRANDMOTHERS carrying into action, from LA to Philly, the very characteristics I read about in scriptures, even with my own Grandmothers. My mother's mother went far beyond just catering to those whom we knew, those who looked like us, those related to us, or those who lived like we did or where we did. My travels with her led me into places where on my own I would not have gone or wanted to be, amongst people who did not like me. Her home was filled with people of every hue, from every community, and even from every continent. She was a living example of what 'social justice' looks like and is.

What is social justice? Well, for me, today, with all the harsh realities of this cold world, I know what it should be, looks like and feels like. There is no better proof of social justice than the quintessence of Christianity, Islam, Buddhism, and 'Way of Life' of our aboriginal native Indians, "Try to do unto others as we wish that others should do unto us." No one will be a faithful believer/adherent student of social justice until he/she loves his/her neighbor as he/she loves him/herSELF.

Expect no one to give you social justice while carrying into practice the extending of social justice to others First!

My Grandmother taught my mother how to fight for me. Almost thirty in, now, I'm learning to carry into practice fighting for my mother and her mother, whom both have passed.

Freedom and Social Justice must exist within FIRST! That's why we fight. That's why we never give up the fight.

The last part of herstory/ourstory my mother shared: "So remember, you started out in the struggle and will remain, but that you are a conqueror." Which I, today, share with each and every one of you.

SOCIAL JUSTICE MUST BEGIN FROM WITHIN STOP LOOKING FOR SOCIAL JUSTICE OUTSIDE OF YOURSELF!

Lamont Harrell
Behind Enemy Lines

If you don't know who you are, any history will do
— **Afrakan Proverb**

I have been incarcerated behind enemy lines since 2007. When I look at the term social justice, the first thing that comes to mind is fairness, impartial behavior, and equality for all people no matter your race, class, gender, ethnicity, culture, or religion. I wish this was true in Amerika, but it's not, because the only people social justice applies to is the dominant society which happens to be Europeans (white people).

Growing up in Baltimore city as a child was rough because my neighborhood was a war zone infested with drugs, violence, prostitution, and dilapidated housing. The level of poverty forced people to do whatever they had to do in order to survive. When I went to school most of the teachers didn't care if you passed or failed because their pay rate wasn't what they thought it should be. On top of that, all the books had pages missing and all the other materials were outdated and ragged y. It was very hard to learn anything in that type of environment. I, as a child, was confused because every-time I turned on the television I saw a different Amerika where Europeans were living in healthy clean communities that were not infested with drugs, violence, prostitution, or dilapidated housing. Their children went to better schools that had brand new books and other materials that made the process of learning easier.

I've always asked why Black people's plight was so different from white people, but I never got an answer until I came to prison and started practicing Pan-Afrakanism. Once I was introduced to the Pan-Afrakan lifestyle, I started studying Our-Story, which is the true history of my ancestors and all the freedom fighting warriors and revolutionaries who fought for social justice and equality. Studying our-story helped me gain a deeper understanding of my people's struggle here in Amerika and abroad. Here in Amerika brothers and sisters from Afrakan descent have been experiencing social injustice for hundreds of years. It's been a constant struggle for Black people to truly be ourselves due to this unnatural environment. Amerika, since the enslavement of Afrakans, has perpetuated violence, negative behavior, and a selfish way of thinking centered around capitalism and materialism. It also promotes alienated spiritual/ religious doctrines along with an educational system that's geared towards the indoctrination, manipulation, and control of Afrakans and other people of color. Each one of these denominations are racist in nature because they are controlled by the dominant society which happens to be rooted in white supremacy. Due to Black people lacking the true knowledge of our story, we fall victim to the institutions within the system just to be accepted by the dominant society, while, at the same time, looking for a savior for the struggles we face every day. Our great ancestor Marcus Garvey once said, "A people without the knowledge of their past history, origin, and culture is like a tree without roots." Black people will continue to suffer from social injustice until we gain the true knowledge of ourselves and start to implement principles such as (Umoja) unity and (Ujamaa) cooperative economies within the fabric of our communities.

Miseducation is the root cause of injustice, starting with the school system. The western educational system is constructed around a European curriculum designed to advance Europeans by falsifying and distorting information to make them feel superior over Afrakans and other melanated people. The system is also designed to disenfranchise, and marginalize Black children so they will grow up being consumers and working for our oppressors instead of being creators, builders, entrepreneurs and business owners. The only way Black people will obtain social justice in Amerika is if we keep fighting against the system of oppression and white supremacy until it's destroyed.

This is going to take (Ujamaa) collective work and responsibility from everyone who claims to be against social injustice, and for freedom, justice and equality for all.

Our struggle continues!

Dewitt Faulkner

Separated and Segregated

On June 13th, 1980, my parents would name me Dewitt Antoine Faulkner after my father's friend. On December 7th, 2004, I became an inmate 398508. In Wisconsin's prison system, many captives would be addressed over the years as inmates, prisoners, offenders, and now "person in our care." PIOC's. I guess the D.O.C., Department of Corrections, wanted to make us feel more like humans, though this "decency" is questionable. In Wisconsin this is the only state that still holds "Truth in sentence." This is an act and bill passed by conservative leaders that says if you're sentenced to 150 years, whether that crime deserves that much time or not, you are expected to do every day of your sentence. The only way around that is if you die in prison by some natural death, die by a virus such as COVID-19 or sickness, or some miracle occurs by something divine. Depending on where you are in Wisconsin's country, town, section, and community, the law seems to be applied differently. For example, if a young Black person of color decides to sell drugs in their community, such as marijuana less than 500 grams, he will become a felon, sentenced from 6 months to one year with extended supervision. This happens even if all of it is for reasons of making a little extra money to feed his or her children. As a person of color his sentence will be harsh. There are no programs or anything to help them better themselves. On the other hand, a young white person of the same age can get arrested, possessing other contraband, and it's a high chance that he will never see the inside of a courtroom jail. Or, if he is sentenced with a term it will be light, consisting of concessions after concessions, programs, treatment, or assigned community services no longer than 72 hours.

I'm writing this essay on "social justice," and what it means to me. Equality, justice, social community, fairness, and rightness. It also means impartial dialogue of the classes, acceptance, and freedom. It does not mean bias against a person's skin color, religion, belief, or gender. Social justice is not oppression, murder, nor derogatory.

Rodney King once asked, "Can we all get along?" In 1991, on March 3rd, Rodney King, a felon, led police on a high-speed chase in the streets of Los Angeles. King, allegedly intoxicated and uncooperative, was brutally beaten by L.A.P.D. officers Laurence Powell, Theodore Briseno, and Timothy Wind. A concerned citizen, who felt disturbed by the police brutality, who heard King scream and beg officers for his life, recorded the horrific sight. That video was released after the police beat King with batons, humiliated him, spit on him, and kicked him. Rodney King eventually was released, and the so-called charge of resistance was dropped. The officers involved with the vicious beating, along with sergeant Stacey Koon, were indicted by a grand jury. I remember the uproar in Los Angeles surrounding this indictment, and then Judge Stanley Weisberg granted a change of venue, moving the trial out of LA county to Simi Valley, a Ventura County. In April 1992, the jury found these nasty officers "not guilty on all counts except on one assault charge on Officer Powell." The assault charge on Officer Powell ended up with a hung jury. The acquittals pissed off most, if not all, of the Blacks in my community.

In 1992, I lived in Hawthorne, CA, an area of Los Angeles County. I remember LA going up in flames. Blacks rioted all over, and not just on Normandie and Florence Boulevard, where Reginald Denny, a white truck driver, was beaten with a brick upside his head in retaliation. I can admit I was afraid for my safety and my family's safety from those who partook in destroying our community.

I once read on the walls: "Fallen Angels, the good die young." There were many names on the walls. What was crazy to me is none of these young people of color made it to see twenty-one years old. The Bible says God kicked out of heaven a number of "Fallen Angels." I always took these angels to be the Lost Angels of Los Angeles. Seeing what was happening everywhere in LA, my cousin told me you either stand and fight, you either ride or get rode on. At 12 years old, I chose to ride.

One day, while me and my homeboy was walking down Rosecrans and Doty Avenue during the four-days of rioting, we saw another one of my homeboys getting jumped by some Mexican gang members. More pulled up on me and my homeboy Buddha, with bats, brass knuckles, and a gun. Taught by my peers (gang member friends) to not run from a challenge but attack first, we just started rushing these guys with fists and kicks. We were able to get the other guys off our homeboy. Other Blacks began to participate in this fight. After it was over, I'll always think about Black folks attacking anyone not Black no matter if you were Korean, Mexican, or white.

I've always known LA to be separated and segregated. The North is where White people lived, in the downtown area, North Hollywood, South Central. Westside and Eastside was made up of Tongans, Latinos, and African Americans. The east side is majority Hispanics, and the rule was if you weren't Hispanic stay away, at least after nightfall. Living in Hawthorne, I attended Yukon Intermediate School. I would get into verbal altercations with this gang member about something disrespectful that was said about one another. I really can't recall because it was stupid. The outcome would be me retrieving my father's gun and utility knife and bringing it back to school with me the next day. I told a friend of mine named K.C. who decided it was ok to tell the entire school. An hour or so later cops would enter my classroom and search my bookbag. They found the weapons. I was handcuffed and placed under arrest. This Hispanic guy must've known what I had because he was planning to do some harm to me. He had weapons also and a gang waiting on me after school. We both were placed in the Patty Wagon's police van and taken to jail. Somehow, I was put on probation until I turned 18. If I got in trouble before then, I would do time in Juvenile detention. Let me add: the gun was a B.B. gun. I had gotten it after my Father decided to take me to live down south.

In Memphis, Tennessee, the environment was very different. No tropical trees, sky blue oceans or heavy traffic and helicopters. I didn't see in 1996 any variety of ethnic groups or races. I saw more white people than I have ever seen in my life. Black folks spoke differently and always addressed adults and elderly people as "yes sir" or "no sir." But like in California, we used the word 'cuz or 'blood and even the derogatory "nigga" when interacting with one another. In the South, southern hospitality was extended to visitors, but I never accepted the racist word, "boy" to address folks here. "Boy," seems to come out of the mouths of both races. In my mind "Boy" was worse than calling me a nigger, a word to degrade Black people.

I'm like the sixth generational descendent of a slave and fourth of a sharecropper and field worker. Social equality and economic justice remind me of a story told down to me from my father about my great-great-grandfather Jesse Faulkner. He was the son of a former slave we call "Grandpapi" because we never knew his name. One day after a long period of labor, Mr. Jesse Frank was wrapping things up getting to turn in for the night, but first had to turn in his cotton so he could get paid. My great-great-grandfather knew how to count and knew when he was getting ripped off or cheated. The folks who paid for his share of cotton tried to cheat him, thinking maybe he was ignorant or probably just acting plain "evil." When my great-great-grandfather questioned this white man about the monies which were missing, they got into a heated discussion, and my great-great-grandfather was shot in the head point-blank with a shotgun. The sound scared the horse, its reins wrapped around my great-great-grandfather's neck, and his horse dragged and pulled him, reaching home. His wife and kids witnessed this. The youngest who saw it was my grandfather. There were no consequences for the action of this white man.

It's written in our Constitution that equality and justice is for **all**. But it's really only for some. Today we fast forward to all of the civil monuments, NAACP, Black Lives Matter, but nothing major has changed. We Blacks in America are still getting hosed down, dog's sic on us, over sentenced, and murdered in cold blood. Today, we see racism, discrimination, and cowardly attacks of immigrants and Asians. Hispanics are being 'stored' in facilities because they chose to seek help, believing in the ways of America, land of opportunity and freedom.

I'm serving a 70-plus sentence for a crime I didn't do. I watch and read about my fellow whites getting less time, slaps on the wrist for far worse crimes than for which I was allegedly "convicted." If I had been white, a female, and older, I wouldn't have ever experienced what I've been through: injustice. Even being incarcerated I still experience harsh treatment, injustice, and bias because of racism and social injustice. We must do better as a society, community, and become anti-racist, have dialogues, and promote justice and social equality. Love first for it's the key to harmony. Finally, Justice for George Floyd. He can rest in peace and until we get justice for all of "Them," wrongful convicted Black men must keep the faith.

Stay strong. All in the dark will come to light. Our time will come.

Andre Furtado

Social Food Chain

My name is Andre Furtado, but I am known here, in prison, as number F84784. Ironically, for the CEOs of this prison system, numbers are also important, because that is the profit margin or their bottom line. Before I delve into deeper thoughts and concepts, I'd like to briefly share my background. I'm 34, from Santa Cruz, and of mixed race. My mother is Portuguese. My father is "Black." I entered a world that is colored with injustice and racism! My mother's well-off, home-owning family literally threatened to cut her off if she went through with the pregnancy of a Black boy. Funny how they do not completely see me as part of their family, not just Black. Can you imagine a 6'4" 240 lbs man crying in prison? Well, as I write this, the realization of my creation has made me emotional.

I will say my mixed race essentially gives me a conflicted view on life and everything in it. Both the slave and the slave master run in my DNA. Am I to choose which defines me?

If you ever want to know the direction of America and what Americans are into, you look at what America is giving tax breaks/deductions for. Follow the money. A key issue in our social system is that the rich don't mind that many are poor and starving. The privileged racists at the top of the social hierarchy don't mind that many people are discriminated against. The lower class has been targeted to fill up the "for-profit" prison system. The statistics have shown that since the days of slavery, crimes committed by Blacks were punished, and punished harshly. While a specific "class" killed, raped, and whatever else they chose with immunity. What has changed? Rhetoric? Nice guys in nice suits literally doing what they please at our expense.

The problems that I see in society have solutions. But before stating those solutions, the problems must be defined. Recently, I experienced a travesty of a court proceeding by Santa Clara County. My rights were violated, as well as my due process and my right to a fair trial. I was offered a 3-year plea deal. Because I believe in my innocence, I refused and I was sentenced to 104 years to life for pimping my girlfriend. This happened even though she came to my trial and said that "she lied" and the charges were false and should be dropped. She only said that stuff to incriminate me out of anger.

I've personally experienced social injustice in the very thing that is supposed to represent justice, our justice system. Am I the only one? Hardly. I am one of many who have faced such injustices. People of color, lower class and the underprivileged have essentially become "prey" to the predators. Our system has become a social food chain. However, we humans are one! One group, one class, and one race regardless of our color, our hair, or whichever body of water we've come across from. In time, we will learn.

There is a group of elites who "know" what the one thing that separates us is. A few of us are sent from God/Universe/Stars to teach and grow and direct us into a closer version of God called profits. The elite hide information, as they thirst for more information to further muddle and twist up that information. We know that people today are being divided by their class or income more than race. Racism will die hard because hate of it has entered people's DNA. To combat social injustice, we must connect. We must protect others. We must respect all! It starts with us! Because if we wait for them to change, we will continue to wait until the end of times.

As I sit in this cell, it's a daily fight not to become institutionalized. A fight I will not lose, because once the prison system succeeds in institutionalizing one, you are a default, an invalid. I also find it difficult at times to fit into my surroundings as I rarely share interest or common thoughts with the populace. But we are by nature social creatures. As a plant needs water and sunlight, we need each other to bloom and flourish as the heavens intend.

However, social injustices don't end in prison. Some correctional officers are taught or find it in themselves to treat humans locked up in prison like slaves and second-rate humans. Correctional officers, like police officers, exert control and power – displaying the predator versus prey relationship further.

Undeniably, as humans our beliefs, concepts, and perceptions dictate the colors we use to see the world and the people in it. The youth are the determinant factor. So we must provide an openness, oneness, correctness. Better schools and youth programs are integral. I lived in Oakland when I was six years old. I'll never forget the 20-30 minutes I walked to school; I passed twenty liquor stores, which were nearly on every corner.

We cannot sabotage or sacrifice one group of people without eventually suffering and paying the price also. We must mimic a flower and grow together towards the heavens, and we must collectively open our minds, petal by beautiful petal.

Troy Glover

Shame

My earliest encounter with Social Justice resides in my memories of my grandfather. At 10 years old, I would accompany him on his grass cutting routes. My world consisted of two square miles of neighborhoods cluttered with houses and cars lining dirty gravel-top roads. The neighborhoods where he cut grass had houses that were large and spacious. Bright, shiny cars were parked in driveways or garages and the streets were clean and paved. These neighborhoods were only twenty minutes away, yet it felt like I had entered a whole new world, like I was going on an epic adventure.

Another miraculous change I would witness was the transformation of my grandfather. A somber, quiet, and reserved man became jubilant, talkative, and outgoing. It was through him that I learned my "yes suh, and no suh, yes missus and no missus."

I sensed during those outings that my grandfather's attitude towards those white people went deeper than an employee's respect. There was something different about white people that required my grandpa to give more of himself, or so he thought. And so I grew up not really knowing what that thing was, yet I imitated my grandfather's behavior. The world helped to re-enforce my actions as well.

At the age of 13, I spent the summer with my aunt up in Austin. I had met a group of white kids at the local swimming pool who decided to go shoplifting at the store across the street.

Upon getting caught, only I,the Black kid, went to jail. Then at the age of 16 a white classmate and I got caught cheating during an exam. Once again, upon getting caught, only I, the Black kid, got suspended. Lastly, at the age of 19 a fellow service member was caught using a racial slur towards me and, even though he was reprimanded, it was I who was transferred to a different base. These were little incidents in themselves, yet they had a major impact in my life.

I started to develop an unconscious shame for who I was.

I started fantasizing about being white. I detested the neighborhood I grew up in, the music I listened to, and the food I grew up on. I was angry at my own skin. I did everything I could to become accepted in white society. I consciously believed that if I spoke with bass in my voice, acted more conforming and looked less intimidating I would be accepted into that secret society where the world had showed me that life, liberty, and the pursuit of justice actually existed. There was no social justice for my grandpa so how could there be any for me?

Even today, it is difficult to remove the weed of social injustice from my subconscious. If I need a word spelled or if I'm seeking information on a historical event, I find myself seeking the knowledge of a white man. And the world continues to water those weeds by showing how whites here in prison suffer less reprisal from challenging administrative policies than Blacks who challenge the same rule.In addition, I've observed Black inmates compelled to take what is deemed as rehabilitation classes (which isn't a bad thing), yet only whites are readily accepted into the vocational and educational courses. Charles Miller once wrote, "Blue collar-criminals apply no more intelligence than those who are conned by telemarketers." So why would whites qualify for college easier than their Black counterparts? Social justice.

Equality and equity are the love children of social justice because they administer to the education and health of a community. That is how cultural identity and self-identity begins. By incorporating social justice into society we distribute justice adequately, fairly and equitably producing people that can see themselves not as inferior but as equal– achieving life, liberty, and the pursuit of happiness that was never hidden in a false society.

Cedric Brumfield

"Justice"

1

I was born in Oakland, California on November 24th, 1976. However, from the fourth grade up until the second semester of my sophomore year in high school, I lived in Portland, Oregon. For most of middle school and high school I was bussed to a predominantly white school located in Cresham, a suburb of Portland. At first blush, I thought that all of this occurred because of the fact that I obtained one point shy of a 4.0 GPA.

Thanks to Saturday school, that was sponsored by the National Urban League and the Black United Fund, as well as my mom, who took me to the Multnomah County Public Library (that was at the time walking distance from the apartment we stayed in), I was able to read various books. I viewed documentaries and listened to my mom tell me of her personal experiences growing up and as a teenager. This is when the bus boycotts, freedom marches, lunch counter sit-ins, freedom rides, and the Civil Rights Act of 1964 took place . **It was brought to my attention that people who didn't even know I would exist, had paid a great price for me to enjoy progress.**

At the same time there was opposition paving the way for the new Jim Crow, known as mass incarceration, or slavery by another name.

2

I was victimized with micro aggressions known as The Pipeline to Prison, first by way of suspension for the slightest offense of defending myself from being assaulted and called "nigger" and "tar baby." I was then placed in a special behavior class, then in an alternative school, until I simply dropped out of high school in my junior year.

As I look back and reflect on my own experiences, along with the history of the struggle for equality, I am well aware of the fact that the struggle continues. I, too, must do my part, take up the baton, and spend the rest of my life striving for social justice.

3

Social justice, from my viewpoint, and the understanding that I have come to after studying, researching, reflecting and observing my life experience, is an ideal that makes everything equal and fair for everyone that makes up what I like to call the overall human family.

I, Cedric Jamal Brumfield, Black, or African American according to my birth certificate, have never really experienced just and fair treatment. History books, as well as older people, testify to the fact that the struggle for fairness and equality that existed for black people in America then, also continues now. I do not have to use a separate water fountain or eating establishment nor am I relegated to the balconies at main theatres.I don't have to sit in the back of the bus or experience lynching in certain parts of the country. However, the mental, emotional, and physical struggle is still there.

4

I've made and taken time to study, research, and investigate the struggle for equality by way of various books that have given me different views, as well as looking at my own life to form my own perspective. What I have experienced is the new Jim Crow, and also slavery by another name.

5

I, Cedric Brumfield, 247573, did not grow up seeing close and personal social injustices like that of the freedom marches, or of Emmett Till, or of the brothers Martin and Malcolm. **However in my own right I can agree that being black in America was/is a constant struggle, even during the best of times.**
I have read and studied the books that were written about the brothers Martin and Malcolm, and observed the signs of the times that I live in. Mass incarceration is not the only new Jim Crow, or slavery. **It's not a civil rights issue but a human rights issue, because poverty discrimination, as well as lack of opportunity, is a public health disaster and not a criminal justice issue.** The politicians make it out to be one, justifying draconian prison sentences. The derogatory words "nigger," "boy," "coon," and "bafoon" that were used to classify a group of people exist now,in an age of colorblindness, but are replaced with "crime," "criminal," and "felon."

Let's look at the words that are combined to make "social justice." The word "social" by itself is an adjective, characterized by friendly relations, companionship, or connected with fashionable society. It relates to living with others in a community. It is based on status in a society of life, and the welfare of human beings living together in colonies, or hives.

The word "justice" is a noun, defined as the quality of being just (which is an adverb, that can be defined as guided by reason and fairness). It is moral rightness or lawfulness, a claim of what is just according to law. It is the administering of deserved punishment or reward, to act fairly toward, and to appreciate properly. Albert Einstein is quoted for stating that "striving for social justice is the most valuable thing to do in life." I agree. **When looking at the words "social" and "justice" separately, and then combining them into a compound word, they bring an ideal that all of humanity should strive for on a global collective level.**

Corey Jasmin

The Ecosystem of Justice

Justice (Noun): The ideal of righteousness, fairness, and impartiality, especially with regard to the punishment of wrongdoing.

Every man in prison is intimately acquainted with the concept of justice. Every day, the notion of it invades our personal space, much like an illness. The system, which buries us beneath mountains of razor-wire and granite, bases its legitimacy to punish on the dictates of justice. Justice, like the blood of Abel, slain by his brother Cain, cries out with hunger pangs. For the crimes of armed robbery and murder, which I committed when I was only 18, justice demanded I receive a life sentence. And justice got its just deserts.

The ideal of justice, in theory, is a beautiful and noble thing. All men, no matter their color, class, or creed, should be accorded the fairness and equity that are the baseline benefits of being born. That a man will eventually get what he's got coming to him is the foundational premise of karma, the bend of the moral arc of the universe, and God's law of sowing and reaping. Again, this is justice in theory, an un-applied concept.

Applied justice in the United States could not be a more hideous, wretched, and ignoble thing. Justice, specifically criminal justice, has overseen, for example, a disproportionate number of minorities sentenced to death. It has ushered in the mass surveillance and targeting of whole generations, along with the erection of a "gulag archipelago" more gargantuan in scope than anything the Communist regimes in Russia, East Germany, or China could ever chain together.

When my friends and I go to the yard to play basketball, we see faces mostly black and brown and barely any white. We can't help but wonder if, all along, justice was just for us. Our skewed worldview of justice has been shaped more by what it takes than by what it claims to give. The irony of the criminal justice system is that it's designed to procure justice from the unjust. It is justice they themselves have mostly been denied. There is a neglected nexus between criminal justice and social justice. In truth, social injustice creates the kinds of people who become prime candidates for criminal justice.

Social injustice is a common thread that runs through the mosaic of men who live in prison. Their origin stories, much like my own, are rife with episodes of discrimination, deprivation, and degradation regarding housing, jobs, and education. These conditions have so disadvantaged communities of color, multi-generationally, that it has created a type of American caste system, inescapable and inevitable. We are trapped with the foregone conclusions it creates for us all. Left behind, with little hope and limited options, rumbling stomachs grow louder while the voice of reason grows quiet. Crime becomes unavoidable. Indeed, as one of our "founding fathers" has remarked, "A robbery is nothing more than a grassroots redistribution of wealth at the point of a pistol."

When a state does not render justice to members of its most resource-vulnerable population, it becomes an accomplice to injustice. In his "Letter from a Birmingham Jail," Martin Luther King Jr. famously writes, "Injustice anywhere is a threat to justice everywhere." His statement is a commentary on the "interrelatedness of people everywhere," and his belief that "whatever affects one directly, affects all indirectly." Justice, in this respect, is therefore an ideal. It is an ecosystem, one that perpetually requires equilibrium to remain harmonious. When an imbalance of justice arises in this ecosystem, the consequences are unforeseen and harsh corrective measures will be taken to restore balance.

It is difficult for those Americans living cushy and privileged lives to truly empathize with the moral dilemma constantly confronting the hungry, the homeless, and the unemployed. Most Americans are rarely affected. That is, until a member of this underclass, denied social justice, renders injustice to a fellow man through the mechanism of crime. This is not to say that all crime is a result of social injustice.

Much crime is due to the inherent evil, greed, and stupidity which resides in the hearts of men. However, other crimes and other criminals are the derivatives, the blow back. In sum, the chickens are coming home to roost against the discrimination and destitution which plagues our cities.

The phenomenon of injustice begetting injustice is not new. A classic example is the intractable struggle between Israel and the Palestinians. The entire foundation of the state of Israel is built on its victimization at the hands of Nazi Germany. Israel is a society that is forever looking backwards. It is this victimhood, this historically egregious denial of justice which took place during the Holocaust, and Israel's resolve to never again be the victims of such injustice, which undergirds the entirety of their national identity. Sadly, this is also the justification upon which their occupation and victimization of the Palestinians rests. The Palestinians, also perpetually looking backwards to their own victimization and dispossession, have sometimes utilized, in pursuit of their long-denied justice, clearly unjust means (such as terrorism). In this quid pro quo game of retaliation and retribution, neither side has obtained the justice and peace that the past perpetually plays keep away with. All that persists is a never-ending exchange of injustices.

Injustice anywhere is a threat to justice everywhere because of how it seduces victims of injustice to pursue justice through unjust means. Bearing this in mind, it is only obvious that the true key to criminal justice reform is social justice reform. When we, as the Prophet Amos says, "Let justice roll down like waters and righteousness like an overflowing stream," then the forgotten of our land will feel dissuaded from taking justice into their own hands. When social justice is delivered in housing, in jobs, and in education, it will lead to less of a need for criminal justice. Justice will beget justice.

With fervent desire, I look forward to the day when the ecosystem of justice is so balanced, our prisons are empty, and our playgrounds are full.

Leon Fields

Science of Oppression

Oppression is a science, and those who practice it in this country do so with surgical precision.

Consequently, I, Leon Fields R25705, have been a victim of various forms of social terrorism for over forty-four years of my existence. This flagrant subversion of my actualization is a consequence of my phenotype, but to attribute causation to the color of my skin would be self-defeating, as it infers that "I" am amiss. Conversely, culpability lies at the feet of white provincialists due to their insecurities which contribute to their neurosis. As the descendant of enslaved Africans, my struggle is one of "Power": the ability to cause or prevent change. My experiential and historiographical acquaintance with social justice is intimate, which necessitates insightful analysis. My autodidactic journey has been extremely rewarding by equipping me with the requisite tools that allow richer interpretations of life. In absence of such an analytical capacity, my destiny shall follow the masses of Pavlovian dogs or Skinnerian rats.

My journey began in the womb of a Black woman, which at that time was the most dangerous place to be in America for a Black child. Murderous thoughts of infanticide permeated the atmosphere. At this intersection of possibilities more than 30 million potential saviors were killed as a credit to the racist eugenicist, Margaret Sanger. In her words, "The chief obstacles to the normal expression of woman's force are

51

undesired pregnancy and the burden of unwanted children." I thank God for giving my mother the strength to bear me. I too could've been a victim of Planned Parenthood as the strategic genocidal mechanism being placed in my communities.

The primary goal of an education is to provide the student with the ability to cope with tomorrow, in as much as my tomorrow diverges from that of my oppressor and their children. Instead of empowering me intellectually and psychologically based on my unique history, the Chicago Public School system as an institution became a catalytic agent of my demise. Special problems require special solutions. Their so-called neutral curriculum was an exercise in futility. As a descendant of enslaved Africans with specific epigenetic issues I was unwittingly and indiscriminately prodded into imitating my oppressor via the curriculum. The "standard" American education is a major instrument of Euro-American socioeconomic supremacy. Being a special target of hostile white male domination, this essentially was a form of genocidal subjection.

Integration has failed and should be stopped. The U.S. Supreme Court's *Brown v. Board of Education* ruling that segregated schools were "inherently inferior and unequal" was simply wrong. They are unequal when unequally supported. The initial Clarendon County S.C. lawsuit in 1953 only wanted to stop the local board from giving white schools four times as much as they allocated to Black schools, until litigation was taken over by the N.A.A.C.P. Under the auspices of forced integration, white America responded by providing an educational paradigm designed to cause self-hatred in vulnerable and impressionable Black children.

In 1987 I was bussed to a predominately white school in an all-white community. Being one of only four Black males, without any young Black females, my class demographic remained that way through eighth grade graduation. The ambivalence was pervasive every single day.

This arrangement damaged my psyche on so many levels. Until later in life, I didn't fully understand the impact of social inheritance, specifically white middle class. This perceived level of integrated competence as it relates to young white females compounded by the competence of the white female teachers created a situation where my mind unconsciously appraised Black females at a value below their actual worth. Consequently, I've spent decades recovering from the substantive trauma created by this experience. I needed to re-learn how to value and appreciate Black women.

The vast majority of K-8 teachers are middle-class white women, most of whom lack the adequate psycho-social conditioning to bring out the best in Black children. None of them ever informed me that, based on my historical experience, my responsibility was to reacquire the power which had been usurped from me. She never informed me that I needed to develop the fortitude to be able to swim upstream. That I needed to become more resilient because society is malignant. This was complete dereliction of duty, but this is how the system is designed.

Black children love their relationship to their teachers, and they can become catalysts for our education.   But I could feel her apathy and its vibrational energy emanating from her. In some cases, maybe the cultural deficit was too steep to overcome for most of my white teachers, or maybe they just didn't care enough. Reasons aren't excuses. Indifference is a spiritual disease of the heart. I later learned that the sensory apparatus of people exists on a contrast scale. Even though our Black teachers were few, we were able to compare the two and feel the shift of force. As a result of the white teacher's apathy, I've witnessed a few of my peers develop what I now understand as disliking distortion, where we have a tendency not to learn appropriately from someone we dislike. The powerful psychological tendency has altered the trajectory of the lives of countless Black children.

I distinctly remember the depressive movements elicited during insufferable history lessons as I was being indoctrinated with slavery as the nexus of my existence. There was nothing nostalgic in the curriculum for me. Illumined pictures of "Great White Men" lined the books, walls, and halls, along with their great accomplishments. Contrast these powerful images with those of the gloomy, worn, despondent features of Black leaders devoid of any happiness during their perpetual struggle against oppression till death. The intent was to create an impression. The impression that "whites" are the gods of the earth. They are the standard for which we should all strive. An educational paradigm that Hitler would've been proud of had he prevailed. I was given keys to doors that won't open for me. Taught to believe that the world was benign, but in reality, my world is full of contradictions. Where is justice in that?

There are some controversial statements in this essay, like anti-abortion sentiments, but Fields' is strongest in his last paragraph. This essay would do well with a companion piece, either from a woman's perspective regarding pregnancy and raising a Black child, or a commentary piece on the critiques of Brown v. Board from the Black community, or racism in American public schools post-Brown.

Ben Matthew Martin

To Whom it May Concern

To whom it may concern,

First and foremost, I'd like to thank you for taking the time to read this letter of interest pertaining to the ISU UC program. My name is Ben Matthew Martin, and I am currently incarcerated, serving a mandatory minimum sentence of life without parole (LWOP) for the offense of murder, which I took full responsibility for during my initial court proceedings. In other words, yes, I am guilty of the crime that put me in the California prison system. However, luckily for me, this state believes in rehabilitation, and I have made a conscious decision to take full advantage of that fact with the hopes of getting the LWOP sentence reduced, enabling myself the opportunity to earn suitability for parole.

Proponents of mass incarceration are right to argue that crime needs to be dealt with through punishment, but they exaggerate when they claim that locking a person away and throwing away the key is the solution. On the one hand, I agree with society that my past actions warrant prison time. But on the other hand, I still insist that I am capable of correcting my behavior by changing my mentality from ignorance, to an insightful socially conscious law-abiding citizen.

As a result of my realization, I determined that the only way to evolve into a new and improved version of myself would have to be through the process of pursuing education. Fast forward three and a half years since my arrival at Ironwood State Prison (Blythe, Calif.), a prison that is known for their college program. I will have over one hundred units at the end of the Fall 2021 semester. I will have an A.A. in Liberal Arts with Areas of Emphasis in Arts and Humanities, Social and Behavioral Sciences, Mathematics and Science, Business and Technology, and I am two classes away from not only an area of Emphasis in Psychology, but also Sociology. This same time next year, I will have completed the requirements for an A.S. in Business Management, all my coursework will have been done through Palo Verde C.C.

My next steps are to obtain an Alcohol and Drug Studies Certification through the same college. Ultimately, I plan on earning everything Palo Verde has to offer. My goals challenge the thoughts of those critics who have long assumed that all incarcerated individuals are incorrigible and lack the drive and dedication to better understand the reasons for their actions. I am determined to seek the knowledge of education throughout the entirety of my incarceration. Furthermore, another goal is to demonstrate that I've taken the time and initiative, focusing on rehabilitation to the point of being found suitable for parole.

So far, I've been talking about crime, punishment, rehabilitation, and my educational credits earned while incarcerated. But the real issue here is that I want to be part of the Underground Scholars Initiative while still incarcerated. I am trying to find a college that will embrace my educational goals while at the same time understanding and working with the fact that I am currently incarcerated. Ever since learning about USI on the institution's educational channel, I no longer feel marginalized in terms of how far my God-given abilities can take me. I've been saving the contact information for quite some time, and I've finally reached the point of initiating dialogue with USI.

I can imagine how my immediate circumstances may present a challenge for the college, and that correspondence courses may be given only on a case-by-case basis. Even though my incarceration includes a hindrance toward reaching my educational goals, I wholeheartedly believe that USI is furthering the interest of justice by extending their program to me, while in my position.

In conclusion, I am asking for help on a pathway of higher learning. I think that failing to plan is planning to fail, and because I accept my fate as a percentile of a statistic that settles with LWOP, my mindset is focused on handling my business in order to earn parole. In applying myself into that process, I am an example of system-impacted. To take my case in point; the difficulty of obtaining employment at 55-60 years of age and not having, at the very least, a Bachelor's degree, is a different extreme of system-impacted. What I am trying to say is not that finding employment will be impossible, but that the quality of my employment will definitely directly reflect the fact that I have spent 25-30 years in prison without a Bachelor's degree.

I think that my case deserves to be given serious consideration mainly because of my willingness to immerse myself into the process of commitment and conscious effort. Please contact me with input of what I need to do, or whom I should ask for an opportunity. With all that having been expressed, I will go ahead and excuse myself.

SM Steele

From Cradle to the Cell

I came to prison as a child.

At sixteen-years-old I was on adult turf with a knife in my hands, hoping nobody tried me. Walking through the door was hard. My last memory was going to my eleventh grade Spanish class to see my girlfriend, Paulena. But now I was walking into a dayroom full of grown men who stood around ready to kill at any moment.

I heard stories before I arrived. People who I was chained next to on the prison bus warned me.

"Don't let nobody say anything crazy to you."

"Watch out for the guys who stare at you with a sparkle in their eye."

"Don't accept anything from anybody for free."

They told me everything they could think of that I could use to keep myself safe. Did I listen? Yes. That's why I was standing on adult turf with a knife in my hands hoping nobody tried me. Could I do it? Could I stab someone if they tried me? Yes. But would I, became a whole other scenario.

Having these thoughts running through my head was terrifying. Why did I have to think like this at sixteen-years-old? Why was I surrounded around all these grown men ready to defend myself at the blink of an eye? I'm sure it was any mother's nightmare for her child. No mom could imagine her baby boy standing in prison around career criminals, ready to die at any moment. But there I was. And unfortunately for me,

I had no mom to worry about me. She had died when I was six, killed in a neighborhood that is burned into my memory to this day. Sometimes, when I lay in my cell all I think about is what my mom would have thought when she thought about me being locked in a prison with adults.

This was my first time ever being locked up. I had never been in trouble with the law before. And I knew nothing about the law to find out if I had been treated fairly. I was a sitting duck. I had no help neither. My family knew nothing about the law, and we didn't have any money to hire the help of somebody who did. So as usual for a Black Male ensnared by the system, I had to sit in the courtroom with my head down as the judge sentenced me to thirty years to life. It was the fate of a lost child who had gone astray. A lost child who was given a lot in life and had to suffer the consequences. It didn't matter if I didn't choose my parents or communities. It didn't matter if I didn't choose my schools or the people I ended up around. I was responsible for whatever I became even if I didn't know better and that's how the adults in the courtroom saw it.

And that's how the adults in the dayroom at the prison saw it too. It was every man for himself. Well, every child versus every man for himself. The only thing I was expected to do was fight or go out like a sucker. I chose to fight.

My first test came while I was mopping the floor. All I was doing was my job. I was a porter. My job was to keep the dayroom clean. But on this particular day, as I mopped another guy chose to walk over my wet floor. I gave him a pass several times, but when he kept walking back over the floors after I had just mopped over his footsteps, I had had enough. I told him we had to fight. And fight we did. But I found myself wondering why I had to fight over a wet floor. Yet the answer was common sense: Respect.

In prison, RESPECT is the key to survival.

If you make people respect you, you'll find yourself in less trouble. The problem with this, though, is that you'll find yourself in trouble with the law. It's a catch-22. You earn your respect amongst your peers and get left alone but find yourself in and out of solitary confinement. Or you turn out like a sucker, lose respect from your peers, and find yourself in a world of trouble every time you turn around. Either way you go its drama. But the better route in prison is to earn your respect amongst your peers. This is the social dilemma behind bars.

Is this a Social Justice issue? For sure. Children should not be placed in prison to have to figure out how to become the lesser of two evils. Yet many children find themselves stuck in this cycle every day. And it seems that nobody cares. From politicians to prison officials, there is no outrage about children being placed in prison with adults.

Now, twenty-one years later, I look back and I see how hard I had it as a child and all I want to do is fight for juvenile justice. I know I didn't know better at the age of sixteen. I know that I hadn't even lived life. Yet I was eligible to fend for myself amongst adults. I find that unfair. Although I happened to be one of the young guys who fought for his respect, I had to see a lot of young guys get taken advantage of because they couldn't fight for themselves or weren't strong enough.

My call is to Free Children who've been locked behind bars. They deserve a second chance because they never had their first.

Dominique Williams

When Is Enough Enough?

Prison is the most tormenting time of my life. I've had to witness events I will never forget. I've seen correctional officers (c/o's) abuse their authority without being held accountable. I've experienced a separation from my family and friends that has caused me tons of pain and suffering. And I have been treated less than human for a countless number of years.

My very first day in prison, I was sexually forced to strip naked by correctional officers while I was in a room filled with ten other grown men who had been stripped naked as well. The thought of that still haunts me to this very day. For example, a c/o forced me to turn around, lift my feet, wiggle my toes, and to bend over naked ninety degrees to spread my buttocks. Then, I was forced to turn back around, lift my penis and testicles, and run my fingers through my mouth. Finally, after being sexually abused by the c/o, I was able to put on my clothes before being sent to another room.

In the next room, all I heard was the sounds of loud clippers screeching and echoing down the hallway. Then I could hear the sounds of grown men huffing and puffing as they stood next in line to have their hair cut off. As they stood in line, correctional officers laughed hysterically outside the door. Now me, I am Rastafari, so the thought of me being forced to go against my livity had chills running down my spine. My body shook in fear as I had to wait next in line. All I was thinking about was how I was going to explain my religion to them and hoped that the correctional officers would show me mercy because, as a Rastafari, we do not cut our hair. But it would be to no avail. Less than thirty minutes later they shaved my head bald.

But shaving my head bald turned out to be just the beginning of my worries. The next thing I had to face was c/o brutality. I had been accused of having marijuana on me. The officer had given me a direct order to get on the ground. Before I could get on the ground, an officer jumped onto my back and started spraying me with mace. While the first officer was on my back spraying me, another officer ran up and started spraying me, too. I never had a chance to comply with the officer's instructions. I was attacked before I could do the right thing, and after the incident was over I was placed in "the hole" with mace marinating inside my eyes. The pain was excruciating. But more so I was upset because I had been attacked by guards after they made it seem like I didn't comply with their orders. This incident has bothered me for years.

But nothing bothers me more than being separated from the people I love. Separation from my family and friends over the years has caused me great pain and sorrow. At times it has caused me to fall into deep states of depression. The more time that went by away from my family and friends, the more the saying "out of sight, out of mind" echoed through my brain. I started to hear less and less from them as time went by and that caused me to feel alone and non-existent to the free world. Other times it's very challenging to deal with separation from my family because a lot of them believe I am doing life in prison. Although the judge sentenced me to life, I never accept it inside my mind. I tell myself I am going home every day.

That's why the fight to go home is my biggest struggle. I believe it is a social justice issue to lock a human in a...

[manuscript unfinished]

Ghengiz Temujin

Opposition

What is social justice? It depends on who you ask. For those individuals who believe that they have done no wrong, the social justice system is intact. For those individuals who believe in equality, they are still waiting for social justice.

Social Justice lies in the law of the land. Our humanity should define what is just and proper for all of humankind. It should be clearly understood that one man's justice is another man's injustice. The Civil Rights Movement was birthed by humanity. This was a movement that awakened humanity to social inequality and gave birth to what social justice should look like. However, today, in a country divided, two sets of laws of the land exist. One, for Caucasians, and the other for those who are too dark to pass and, or, have a non-European accent. As we witnessed not too long ago in D.C.. there are two modes of treatment towards two different groups of people. Predominantly Black protesters involved in a non-violent Black Lives Matter Movement were violently attacked and sprayed with mace and pepper spray. Later, in this same District, a mob of White people on January 6th, 2021 bombarded the Capitol Hill building intending to cause harm to others. With that intention, they did cause harm, and had also killed someone in an attempt to achieve these goals. They were met with minimal resistance. They violently attacked officers of the law to accomplish what they set out to do. More pepper spray was unleashed by the violent mob and then by the officers. In the aftermath, there were at least six dead including a police officer. No one was arrested on site and of those apprehended later, they were not charged with any form of murder, including that of felony murder.

It has been noted once or twice that had this mob been Black, then, most likely, the outcome would have been different. Social Justice will not be had until everyone can equate it with equal treatment towards all of humanity. Until the minds of humankind are purged from division and are able to see the next human being as their neighbor, social justice will continue to stand just as a coin does. Two-sided!

We are all asking for Social Justice, and humanity is defining what it should look like. There are those white folk who truly believed all of humankind was receiving fair justice. However, today with cameras continuously rolling, they are upset to find that the opposite is true. The images thrust upon them show the evils men do in the name of justice. The lack of humanity in these individuals has caused a rift in the meaning of social justice. In a country that chastises other countries for the ill treatment of their citizens, it fails to look in the mirror. It is widely accepted that the criminal justice system can kill with impunity a Black, Spanish and or any other non-Causcasian person. In order to change this, humanity must be injected into the heart of social justice, after it has been embedded into the heart of humanity. Humanity's awakening won't be front and center until it is emotionally wrenched from its resting place of solace. Within humanity exists the knowledge of what is just and proper. Humanity understands what it means to be equal and how one human should treat another. Humanity doesn't need a measuring rod to gauge the treatment of a person. Social justice requires that measure to demonstrate that therein lies a problem.

There are two differing opinions of the definition of social justice. There are laws supporting the opposition's outcry. The opposing parties see social justice as a tool utilized to fight the lifestyle that has been forced upon them. Humanity has to break the chains of the mind and expose the heart. For, when it comes to justice of any type, the truth of the matter is, what is the characteristic of that Justice sought? Whether it be social, or criminal, how is that justice defined? As with criminal justice it is more clear cut but the waters have been muddied by those who dictate how it should be applied. In many ways, it has been and is used to help some evade punishment and by the same token, it keeps others confined to it by not applying the same standards. Sadly, this ties in with the outcry for social justice which isn't so clear cut but is clearly evident. Humanity dictates that all humankind should be treated equally but social norms dictate otherwise. If you're not of the right color, class, or socio-economic standing you could find yourself believing in that which law and justice say you are entitled to, but the minds of men set out to deprive you of, for you are not of their circle.

In closing, the outcry for social justice will remain, for it is injustice wrapped in a pretty bow, dressed to conceal the hard truth of a wayward society towards a people. Until the entirety of humanity is riled up, the outcry for justice, of any kind, will always resound.

Tyler Anerson

Crossroads

I am a product of the system. I am Tyler Anerson, Inmate M36799, and I was born into the world destined to fail. My mother was a crack addict at fourteen when she had me. She had two other kids before turning seventeen. DCFS (Department of Children & Family Services) took us from her and put me and my brothers in foster care. They kept one of my brothers in Chicago, IL, our hometown, but moved me and my middle brother to Peoria, Illinois—a four-hour drive away from the family I haven't seen since I was nine years old.

I was put into four different foster homes, each one presenting a different type of hell. The caseworkers left me and my brother to fend for ourselves. Our cries for mercy and compassion fell on deaf ears to our white caseworkers. We finally got adopted in our last foster home, but she turned out to be worse than all our other foster homes combined. She treated us like slaves, beating us with anything she could put her hands on, for small infractions like watching her when she cooked, or watching somebody kiss on tv (even if it was a Disney movie). Feeding us was optional even though we didn't lack for food. We couldn't ask for any of it. Sometimes we went all day just eating once.

I ran away at age fifteen, tired of the way I was being treated and being ignored. Every time I ran away, the police would pick me up and take me right back. Not once did they ask or possibly care about why I wanted to run away all the time. They offered my foster mom assistance on whooping me. In their eyes, they felt more compassion for my adopted mom, who had to put up with the problem Black child. Not once did the police think that she was the problem. Despite all that I still wanted to do, my life went downhill after high school because I lacked the motivation to do the right thing.

I came to a crossroads: Here I am a high school graduate and I have nothing to show for it, surrounded by people who didn't have a diploma but who had more money than the teachers. I was easily influenced by these people because even though they were living wrong, they treated me right. When I had nothing, they gave me everything I wanted: a family. Now that I'm locked up for a crime I didn't commit, they still stand by my side, accepting me because they know I'm not the monster they paint me as. They knew the odds were stacked against me and that what the DA or indictment papers say don't matter because they knew me since I was a runaway fifteen-year-old and they trusted me in their house around their family and kids. I did nothing to break that trust then or now. So, I might not be accepted in a white gated community. But I will always be accepted in my hood because we all we got.

Jacklyn J Price

Keep-away

Justice was created to encourage fairness. But because we're so divided, it has been perverted to something it was never intended to be. Why? Shouldn't there be more than one equitable resolution to satisfy social justice? It's not just about racial equality even though this is where it's most recognized. It's for all people who are underrepresented as a community; being Black just so happens to be at the forefront.

As a kid, I remember going out to dinner with my mother and siblings. We would enter the restaurant before some of the white customers, who were greeted with a smile. We weren't greeted at all; instead we were treated as being a nuisance, an interruption. The white families were served first while my mother had to remind the waitress that we were still waiting to be served. It wasn't until after another few white families received their food that we were allowed to eat. That's when I realized I was put into a specific category, an unimportant category.

We didn't have much money, and it was obvious by the way we dressed. I didn't understand if we were overlooked because of the color of our skin or the social class we identified with. Maybe the waitress knew we could barely afford the food, so a tip wasn't feasible.

There's a children's game called "King of the Mountain." The stronger players' job is to keep the weaker players from taking possession of the top of the hill. This is how society is designed; it separates the players into classes. We have the rich, the poor, and the largest, the middle class. In addition to classes, there is white, black, and gay (also known as the LGBTQ community). We're all broken up into categories. No matter what community we are part of, social justice should be the same.

As an inmate, we're still discriminated against, and not just outside the walls but inside as well. I'm an educated Black woman with several college degrees. I have become fluent with the law and know how to use the law library. I applied to work as a librarian in the law library. I wasn't hired. Instead, they chose an old white woman, barely able to move and with no knowledge of how the law library works.

They told me I could be the orderly who takes out the trash and cleans the toilets. Then, I applied to work in the commissary, the prison store. I didn't get that job either. It's prison policy that an inmate must have at least a G.E.D. to work in the commissary. The position was given to a white woman who has been "trying" to get her G.E.D. for the past two years without serious determination. These are two good departments to work in while incarcerated. Yes, even inmates are discriminated against. How can I become a stronger player when there's a system all around me that's playing "keep-away" with the tools I need to become better and stronger?

Social injustice begins with racial inequality, but it doesn't end there. There's only one equitable resolution to achieve social justice. Race, gender, sexual preference, or political views shouldn't matter;

everyone is the same and should be treated accordingly. Everyone deserves a fair opportunity to fight for the top of the hill no matter what that hill may be.

Mark Barney
A Slave to Hope

I was born in Stockton, California, and raised in a working, poor community of Blacks, whites, Mexicans and Filipinos. My stepfather was an ordained minister employed by the State of California as a custodian. My mother was a homemaker and the strongest, most impressive woman I've ever known.

In 1972, we moved to an inner city community in Sacramento that happened to be the most prosperous Black community in the city. The community boasted a Black-owned newspaper, a taxi cab service, restaurants, nightclubs, car lots, and many other Black-owned and operated businesses. There was also a cadre of Black and revolutionary nationalists that would post literature on boarded up storefronts to raise awareness about George Jackson, Angela Davis, Bobby Seale and others who were being held by the State of California's so called Department of Corrections. This was the environment where I spent my formative years. I was a twelve-year-old thief in training (self-taught) and I loved the opportunities that the city presented.

My first prison stint was in 1982. Inside of the prison walls I encountered Black men striving to deconstruct the miseducation that young Black men had been exposed to in our schools and to educate us in ways that would serve as a vehicle for liberation. Accepting responsibility, holding oneself accountable and looking out for the welfare of the next brother were lessons that were preached daily. Cleanliness in speech and body, situational awareness, self-discipline in study and physical fitness were expected of "conscious brothers." These practices were modeled by the Muslims, Panthers and Nationalist Brothers who were our teachers and guides.

In the California Department of Corrections (CDC) you grow up quickly. A failure to recognize the conniving, treacherous men among you may cost you your life. I see similarities with brothers in our community today. The time has come for the Black men in our communities to have an honest conversation about the pain and suffering that our own conduct is producing. Before confronting institutionalized racism that obviously exists, we may want to address issues within our immediate control. Specifically, the actions of a small minority that insist on destroying themselves and others and the inaction of those among us who have yet to challenge those behaviors (I begin with myself). How can we expect social justice from others when Black men are being unjust to their own family members? While women and children are not safe in their own homes, how can we expect others to provide social justice? We must set limits and decide how far we are willing to go to provide our own with a sense of justice so that those within the community have a sense of security and hope. Will the men in our community sit idly by as women are abused and raped by other Black men or while underage girls are lured or forced into the sex industry? Black "boys" masquerading as men are killing Black children as they involve themselves in childish behavior under the guise of "gangsterism."

One prominent Islamic leader proposed that Black people should pool their resources and buy land to set aside for graveyards within the Black community. He then suggested we proceed through the community and remove those men that insist on living a life of destruction. That may be extreme, but it highlights the need for men in the community to provide a sense of hope for their own people. For those outside of our community, it shows that we are going to be proactive when it comes to seeking justice. I end this with a poem by brother Albert Nuh Washington. A brother that sacrificed his life for the liberation of his people.

Black
is a political condition
a state of oppression and consciousness
a nation seeking to become

                                        a people who hope

Liberation
is freedom from oppression
freedom to define, to determine one's destiny
free from despair

                                             a slave to hope

Army
is a political armed unit
to defend and preserve
after it achieves

                            Liberation for those who hope

Jerrell Brooks

Hands Up

I am a 35-year-old Black man who has been illegally incarcerated since the tender age of 17 for a crime I did not commit. My name is Jerrell Brooks #1120649. I have been convicted of two counts of 1st degree murder and sentenced to die in a level five maximum security prison here in Missouri, home of one of the deadliest gangs in American history: the Ku Klux Klan.

Since I have been in prison, I've found myself and my purpose. During the 19 years I have been here, I have demonstrated a commitment to rehabilitation by not having over 55 points in the Disciplinary Conduct Violation Point System. I have literally completed every program the Missouri Department of Corrections has to offer or require an offender to complete. I've also made a transition from an active gang member to becoming a God-fearing man.

I come from poverty. I grew up in one of the most dangerous cities in the country ill this day, St. Louis. It is a city where most people barely survive to see 17.

My story is a typical one: A poor young Black child growing up in a poor-urban community in America while suffering from some form of abuse (mentally or physically, if not both). I had one big question in my heart, "God, why me?" I never knew my biological father because, he too, has spent his entire life in a Missouri State Prison. I was raised by a single parent, my beautiful mother. I only saw or had a father figure for 3/5 of my entire life, let alone in my household. The majority of those times my stepfather was either struggling with substance abuse or he was abusive towards my mother and myself. I am pretty sure now you can understand how my story goes: Another SELF-DESTRUCTIVE BLACK CHILD turning to the streets looking for love in all the wrong places, you know! I am another statistic to the white man's mass incarceration plot dating back to the year of…forever????

I am from a state home to the most prisons in America, even with states like Texas and California whose populations double if not 3 or 4 times more than ours. If this injustice system in the state of Missouri isn't about the dollar, then how does this happen to a small state like Missouri? People, you would think that with over 20 something correctional facilities here in Missouri that there should or would be more rehabilitation, but it is the total opposite. How do you expect a person that enters the prison system as a teenager at 17 and is released when he is 35-40 years old, to live a productive life when he was given no productive tools of educating himself or even given productive job training skills to prepare to enter back into society? He has been absent from society for so long, he will have to re-learn and adopt, all while hoping that he never re-offends and is sent back to prison.

Do I find this Injustice System and the Missouri Department of Correction a joke? Yes, I do and this is why! There is no rehabilitation or safety anywhere in the system. The word Rehabilitation means: Prepare someone who has been injured, ill, or addicted to drugs to resume a normal life through training and therapy. It means the total opposite here at South Central Correctional Center in Missouri. It is the U.S. government's responsibility to create an environment that will allow prisoners and citizens to live a safe and productive life. The Department of Corrections is more than a set of institutions; it is a state of mind. It is this state of mind which needs to be reformed.

In the U.S. criminal justice system, there is a saying, "once a criminal, always a criminal." I personally beg to differ. A criminal is again, a mind state. A mind state that can be reformed by the simplest thing as being loved by someone or even a visit by someone you love. It's the lack of attention! We also know that every part of the criminal justice system falls most heavily on the poor and people of color, including the fact that slavery is mandated by the 13th amendment of the U.S. constitution asLEGAL SLAVERY!

I am a prisoner who has not seen his mother since June 21, 2009. It's 2021. 12 years! Readers, I would like to tell this brief story of a Black teen whose life was taken by the hands of the Injustice System. On October 6, 2002, at 10:17pm, a 17-year-old Black boy was taken away from the arms of his mother by the hands of two white men (homicide detectives) who entered his home with a "No Knock Warrant." He was last seen wearing dark color jeans and a Block Hoodie. He was 5'8" 140lbs. He had $262 and a pack of skittles in his pocket. He was taken to a dark place where he was held and beaten for two days, screaming and hollering, "Momma, I can't breathe!" But his cries fell on deaf ears, and he received no help.

October 4, 2004, this Black teen stands trial in front of 12 of his supposed peers with his hands up chanting, "Hands up please don't shoot me" and "I'm innocent." Yet, he was still shot and killed by the hands of the Klan: Juries. His body was sent to a morgue also known as a "prison" The Black teen's soul was given to a higher power called God because he was so young and innocent. God said to the boy, "Remain strong, keep faith because one day soon you will RISE and be let out of prison with a new life. These foolish acts brought upon you Breonna Taylor, Mike Brown, Trayvon Martin, George Floyd, will be under forgiven. Continue to pray because everything will be okay."

Amen!

Robert Gillens

What does Social Justice Look Like?

What should social justice look like in an American democracy today? One would at least expect there to be justice for all – no matter what race, religion, gender, age or sexual orientation. However, police brutality and mass incarceration play critical roles in our quest for social justice in America.

The video footage of a group of white police officers beating an unarmed Rodney King on March 3, 1991, went viral. The world watched horrified as men sworn to protect and serve committed heinous acts that were caught on tape by a concerned plumber named George Holiday. Adding injury to the unwarranted attack, an all-white jury acquitted all the cops of any wrongdoing. This led to an uprising in Los Angeles which engulfed the city in flames and ultimately claimed more than sixty lives.

Three decades later, and after numerous unwarranted and controversial police killings of Blacks (Amadou Diallo, Sean Belkl, Kathryn Johnston, Oscar Grant, Trayvon Martin, Rekia Boyd, Mario Romero, Timothy Russell, Malissa Williams, Eric Garner, Laquan McDonald, Tamir Rice, Walter Scott, Freddie Gray, Sandra Bland, Mansur Ball-Bey, Mario Woods, Alton Sterling, Philando Castile, Breonna Taylor, along with so many others), the violence continues. Recently, Derek Chauvin, a white Minneapolis police officer, was criminally charged with smothering unarmed African-American George

Floyd to death by pressing his knee on Floyd's neck. The more than nine-minute incident, captured on a cell phone recording, was Rodney King all over again – but this time on steroids. The recording revealed Chauvin nonchalantly snatching Floyd's life away as he blatantly ignored Floyd's cries of "I can't breathe" more than twenty times. We also heard Floyd calling for his deceased mother. This outraged millions of Americans of all races, and the world united like never before. Around the globe people came together to protest the killing. Together they said: this is wrong; this is unacceptable, America!

The fact remains, we have rarely seen a group of Black or Latinx cops kill an unarmed white person. Is it because they adhere to the rule of due process? Or are they just more careful? Regardless of the reasons, for us to achieve change, we must honestly recognize that racial profiling and brutality by the police is rooted in institutionalized racism that can be traced to the Atlantic slave trade. Since the end of the slave trade, the violence has continued in the form of kidnapping, rapes, lynching, and other brutal crimes whites have committed against the African family. Many often wonder what have people of color done to deserve such long-term hatred? Is it merely because of the color of their skin? After all, the creator chose to create man with various colors, sizes, and characteristics. The audacity of anyone to question their own maker's creation should be more than troublesome.

Solution: because racism and an abuse of authority can be a deadly cocktail, police candidates should undergo ethical, racial and discriminatory training, and thorough background checks before becoming police officers. There also needs to be greater oversight and supervision over police officers. In addition, there must be accountability for officers who choose to violate these ethical regulations. There must be sovereign immunity, civil law amendments and other laws put in place by Congress to end the shoot to kill, or choke to kill an unarmed American.

We have witnessed countless cases where white cops are clearly seen on tape killing unarmed Blacks. However, if they are ever criminally charged, they are systematically acquitted by all-white jurors. Nonetheless, American jurors play a vital role in American's obtaining social justice. Through the criminal justice system, jurors are empowered to be the voice of the voiceless. When jurors, however, fail to convict those blatantly guilty of taking an unarmed American' life, social justice too is smothered to death.

Mass incarceration: American is coined the "land of opportunity." If so, why does America lock up more of its citizens in prison than any other nation in the world? Have we become an aggressive police nation obsessed with encaging our own people? Are we shunning the real rehabilitation that's needed to reform Americans and help them become productive members of our society? Truth be told, mass incarceration sweeps the nation's poorest into a cycle of harsh prison sentences, superficial rehabilitation, excessive catch-22 supervised release, parole and probation terms that lead to more imprisonment.

President Joe Biden has admitted that the 1986 Anti-Crime Bill and the 1994 Crime Bill were among the key factors that led to unwarranted and draconian prison sentences for many Americans, contributing to the country's mass incarcerations problem. Both bills incorporate the "lock-up-throw-away-the-key" approach and the racial disparity in crack-cocaine sentencing laws.

Many ask, why does the federal government have over 98% conviction rate in prosecuting Americans? Any system that is that lopsided is evidence of unfair practices and the lack of social justice. "Our current federal sentencing laws are out of date and often counterproductive," said Republican Congressman Mike Lee from Utah. "We should do as, President Biden has suggested, seek the elimination of mandatory minimum (prison sentences)…We don't have to seek the highest possible offense with the highest possible sentence…legislatively, we should look at equalizing… what's known as the crack powder ratio, which has had an enormously disproportionate impact on communities of color," said Attorney General Merrick Garland at his February confirmation hearing.

Mass incarceration in America will end and when Congress re-examines and reduces the federal and state sentencing guidelines, when it ends ghost drugs conspiracy charges (based on hearsay and other faulty factors) and multiple sentencing enhancements for prior convictions (after prison terms have already been completed), and when it implements a more fair and transparent criminal justice system, where time actually fits the crime. Then, and only then can social justice truly be effective and shine and sparkle across this nation.

Levester J Loggins

One Hundred Steps Backwards

As a young bright-eyed child, I was extremely proud of my family lineage. Just knowing I had something no other kid in my neighborhood had made me feel good inside. I had a grandfather, Jim, who was born in 1900, and I had a father, Elmer, who was born in 1928. They were born in Hayti, a small town in southeastern Missouri.

Not only that, the early 1900s had a significant and special meaning to me. As a child visiting my grandparents' home, I was completely amazed by the amount of farmland they owned. As I looked across their fields, I could not see another house for what appeared to be miles. At that time, I was too young to know or understand anything about sharecropping.

From the 1500s through the 1900s, whites in America enacted various laws that legalized the brutal, violent, and barbaric treatment of Black men, women, and children. I used to sit at my kitchen table, lie on the living room floor, or curl up in my bed listening intently to my parents or grandparents telling me endless stories about their parents and their childhood and what it was like growing up in the era of Jim Crowism.

I would learn later that after slavery was abolished, the early 1900s became an era in which Blacks were not entitled to justice of any kind. As best as I could remember, there were no such stories during my childhood. Neither my parents nor grandparents told me stories about the deaths of Dr. Martin Luther King, Jr., Malcolm X, Marcus M. Garvey, or Emmett Till, or about Black Wall Street or the Klu Klux Klan. Nor did they tell me stories about the treatment they or their parents received at the hands of white people prior to and after the Jim Crow laws took effect.

In fact, my parents and grandparents did everything they could to shield me from the racism and discrimination that existed in America. But the reality was it would have been wonderful to hear their firsthand accounts of the death of Dr. Martin Luther King, Jr., and how they felt about it. Did they agree with King's message and vision for Black survival? More importantly, did they agree with King's "I Have a Dream" speech? How did they feel about Malcolm X and his message for the Black people living in America?

Admittedly, during the early part of America's history, white people staunchly defended their segregationist policies. The policies they enacted meant that Black people could not drink from the same water fountains they drank from. Blacks could not eat at the same restaurants with them. Blacks could not go to school with them. And Blacks could not look at white women.

Even when Blacks formed their own communities and businesses in Tulsa, Oklahoma, white people went in and killed hundreds of innocent black people and burned down their communities [in the Tulsa Race Riots of 1921]. To this date, no prosecutor has investigated the incident, and no one has ever been arrested and charged for that horrific incident. This ruthless treatment of Blacks occurred in America despite the words in the Constitution's preamble saying, "All men are created equal."

As a kindergartener in 1967, I was enrolled at Clark Branch No. 1, a school just two blocks from where I lived. Despite living in a Black neighborhood, I don't remember if

Clark Branch No. 1 was an all-Black school. I definitely don't remember any white children being in my classroom.

After a car accident, my parents moved to a house on the northside of St. Louis, which was deeper in the Black community. While white people did live in our new neighborhood at first, I noticed that they started moving out.

In 1969, I was enrolled as a first grader at Wallbridge Elementary school. Even then, I don't remember if my new school was an all-Black school or if white children went there. But even if they did attend, I believed that the color of a person's skin didn't matter.

By 1970, however, a new reality would flip my world upside down. Apparently, prior to the killing of Dr. Martin Luther King, Jr., racial tensions and strife between Blacks and whites were roaring in America. Discrimination and racial injustice were at their highest point. Legal battles for social justice were being waged around the United States.

The NAACP was very instrumental in fighting for social justice reforms. The legal battle the NAACP waged in response to Rosa Parks' arrest after her refusal to give up her bus seat to a white woman was just one of the many legal battles fought by that organization in an attempt to enact social justice reforms. The appointment of Justice Thurgood Marshall to the Supreme Court further paved the way for the NAACP to argue the illegality of school segregation policies.

At the time, I didn't know anything about the legal battles being fought and won in the courts across America seeking to overturn the country's racist and segregationist policies. My parents never had those conversations with me.

However, in 1970, after I completed first grade, my parents told me that I would no longer be allowed to go to Wallbridge. They said that I would be used across town to attend a white school on the city's south side. As a young child, that made absolutely no sense to me, especially when there was a school in my neighborhood. Besides, a school was supposed to be a school regardless of where it was located. I didn't know at the time that some schools (white) were better equipped than other (Black) schools.

I can't say that I was too happy about having to ride a bus across town just to go to school. But being young, I had to obey my parents. Gratiot Elementary was the first white school I was enrolled in. I completed the second through fifth grade at that school. Wade, a magnet school, was the next white school I was enrolled in. I completed the sixth through eighth grades there. After graduating from Wade, I was enrolled in O'Fallon Tech, another magnet school, where I would do shop work the first half of the day and attend school the second half of the day.

While I was enrolled in white schools, I did the same thing that my parents did. I closed my eyes so I couldn't see any racial or social injustice of any kind. My parents never took the time to tell me about the incident in which the National Guard was called in to prevent a Black student from attending an all-white school.

Being bused to all-white schools had many memorable benefits. At Gratiot in 1972, I met and fell in love with a young white girl named Christine. I was ten years old at the time. Little did I know that seventeen years earlier, in 1955, Emmett Till was brutally murdered for allegedly whistling at a white woman. But I didn't know about that incident. It definitely wasn't taught in school. So Christine remained the object of my desire from 1972 to 1981, the year both of us graduated from O'Fallon Tech.

When I was young, I did not believe that racial and social injustice existed, and people were lying if they said otherwise. Racial injustice did not exist in 1982, when a St. Louis police officer impregnated Laura, a 13-year-old girl, and ended up killing another young girl in an attempt to kill Laura. The policeman wanted to keep Laura from telling her parents that he got her pregnant. But, despite the protest that occurred right after the killing of that innocent girl, I did not see any social injustice in what had happened. To me, killing that innocent girl was just a freak accident. I concluded that had she not been sitting on her front porch, she never would have been killed.

I actually wasn't exposed to the idea of social justice until long after I was in prison. Prior to coming to prison, I totally believed in the American ideology that "All men are created equal," and that under the Due Process Clause of the Fourteenth Amendment no one should be deprived of "life, liberty or property without due process of law." Those were the things I was taught in those white schools and I believed in them.

Since the late seventies and early eighties, however, there was so much injustice going on in and around African American communities that I often found myself crying. Crying because there was nothing I could do about it. Crying because deep down inside I knew something had to be done to correct injustice of any kind. The police beating of Rodney King was shocking, but what was even more shocking was an all-white jury finding the white officers not guilty. The verdict was just a confirmation that white people don't see Black people as being equal. Therefore, they will continue to protect their own even to the detriment of the rights of others.

Even if there were racial issues or social injustices going on in America, I believed for a long time that the enactment of various social justice initiatives and reforms meant that America had outgrown its racist and prejudicial treatment of the people it recognized as fifth-class citizens. However, despite the strides America has made and continues to make in social justice reforms, the events surrounding the 2020 presidential election and the January 6th insurrection only reaffirm that racism, prejudice, and social injustice are alive and well in America.

What kind of social reforms were made in response to the killing of Emmett Till? To the Birmingham, Alabama, Church bombing in which four Black children were killed? To the killing of Trayvon Martin? I am reminded of what the late Malcolm X said: "Black people don't need civil rights, they need human rights." Malcolm X reminded us that civil rights can be stripped away at any time. Just look at the current debate over affirmative action.

Social justice can never be accomplished if America continues to take four steps forward and one hundred steps backwards. As I see it, every effort must be made, even by us prisoners, to ensure that equal social and economic justice is given to everyone. To commit crimes and warehouse ourselves in America's prisons, then cry about social injustice, is counterproductive to the efforts of those on the front line fighting for meaningful social justice reform.

History shows that the small steps towards progress result in giant steps being etched into the annals of history.

Christopher Deon Gattis

In the Mind of a Prisoner

In promoting social justice and confronting prejudice and discrimination, one must look at how their own life is a reflection of race relations in broader society. Growing up in a single parent home, my mom taught us to love, not hate. She taught us to treat people like you wanted to be treated. She never discussed the issue of race with us, even though she cleaned houses for rich white folks. She was their cleaning lady by day, but I saw her as my mom. As a single mother of five, she was willing to hustle any way she could to make sure her kids had everything they needed.

I do not know much about my family history, other than my grandpa Junior was an alcoholic and his son, my father, was a drug addict. My grandma and my mom did not get along. Once a year, family reunions brought our kinfolk together for a day. Other than that, we were strangers from afar. Grandma's view of white folks was stained, behind the memories of Black leaders being assassinated, the enactment of the 13th Amendment, and the denial of voting rights, good paying jobs, and affordable housing. She told us of the sounds of the KKK marching through the streets, bolstering fear, and spewing hate while burning crosses, lynching folks, and raping Black women like it was a sport. She insisted that her shotgun stood by the door, in case one of those "white devils" showed up at her house. Grandma told her grandchildren that they were never to mix bloodlines, or she would disown us.

Although she had a lot of wisdom, I never gave her comments a second thought or an ounce of consideration.

I remember growing up in Greensboro, North Carolina, in the '70s and '80s when rap music had meaning, and the lyrics spoke about poverty in the neighborhood and did not denigrate women like it does now. During this time, you rarely heard about violent crimes being committed and if you did it was a fist fight, not guns. When the crack epidemic hit the streets in the '90s, crime began to rise as more guns and drugs were sold in the Black communities. **Children grew up watching their fathers and uncles mix up cocaine in the kitchen.** By the time they were teenagers, many boys my age had become *runners*, and *lookout boys* for drug dealers. So much money was put in their pockets, it drowned out what educators were trying to teach them. Soon, the school dropout rate increased in the Black communities. Boys were becoming men "faster," and their fathers were being carted off to prison or being dumped in the local morgue. While American soldiers were fighting a war against terrorism, manufacturing jobs were being sent overseas, and the uneducated workers became unemployed. Mothers were giving birth to crack babies, and those who had unprotected sex contracted AIDS (HIV) and other diseases that spread rapidly throughout our communities. People were living in fear that the next terrorist attack could be worse than 9/11, or that a race war could happen any day, due to media reports of acts of violence against people of color. In the past ten years, police killings of unarmed Blacks have spiked, according to the United States Department of Justice. The sad truth is many people don't support the Black Lives Matter movement because they feel it is over-rated, considering you have Black-on-Black murders daily. **But before discrediting the movement or the people involved, you should listen to the people pleading for social justice.**

For the past 7,300 days I have lived behind prison walls working on the issues that got me this sentence of life without parole. When I first entered the "jungle," the population of Black prisoners was significantly higher than whites. Statistics would suggest that the 1994 Crime Bill that President Bill Clinton signed into law targeted the African American community. More time was given out for crack than powder cocaine, meaning more Black men went to prison for longer than white men who could afford the more expensive drugs. Now, this new epidemic of opioid drugs has targeted the white community, and I am seeing a shift in talk toward rehabilitation and drug treatment programs as alternatives to the "lock 'em up, throw away the key" approach that ruled the crack era.

These views remind me of my own trial, which was mired in discriminatory mistakes, such as an instance when the trial judge promised the juror's husband he would rush my trial so they could go on vacation. There was also evidence that my signature was forged on the Miranda Right Waiver form, and the trial judge did not let the jury hear evidence of a struggle over the gun when the autopsy report and forensic evidence revealed the victim had gun powder on their left thumb, right palm, and prints on the barrel and grip of the gun. My court appointed attorneys did not fight for me. An all-white jury heard my case. Since I did not have money to hire a post-conviction lawyer to do my appeals, every court has denied my *Pro Se* motions. North Carolina prisons do not have law libraries, so you must buy your own legal books or rely on others who have them. Many "lifers" are experiencing the same fate I have been dealing with over the past 20 years. **The good news is that I did not let the unfairness stop me from rehabilitating myself!** Through prison programs and correspondence courses, I have completed two college degrees and written and published four books. I facilitate Narcotics Anonymous meetings and mentor at-risk youths, all from behind these prison walls. Recently, the family of the victim of my crime wrote an Affidavit to the Governor of North Carolina asking for clemency on my behalf. When the COVID-19 Pandemic hit, everything got put on pause. As COVID-19 ends, we feel positive that the Governor will look at my clemency request.

On August 16, 2020, my only son was murdered in another senseless act of gun violence. As I was grieving over my son, God reminded me that I must show forgiveness and grace to the person who killed my son, just as my victim's family has shown me. This was a hard pill to swallow, but it allowed me to swap shoes with the people I hurt many years ago. Those who do not understand social justice fail to see the inherent value we have within to make a difference and call to the forefront those issues of racism, injustice, and any effort meant to silence the voices of the oppressed.

Jeffrey McKee

A Feel Good Term for an Ugly Problem

What does social justice mean to me? Good question. No one has any control over the time, place, manner, or circumstances in which we enter this world. Once we arrive our views and opinions are formed and shaped by our surroundings and influences. As time progresses we gain more knowledge and different experiences change our views.

I was born exactly ten years after John F. Kennedy was shot, in Portland, Oregon. I grew up in a middle-class suburb that was predominantly white. There was one Black family in the neighborhood. I remember my parents inviting them over for dinner and being sociable, but they never returned and appeared to keep to themselves. There were only two Black kids that went to my elementary/junior high. Although I did not hang out with them regularly, I considered them friends. There were probably several kids of the LGBTQ community, but none were open about it, nor did I personally care either way. I like to believe that I have always treated others based on their individual character and how they treated me. In reflection, we did play "smear the queer" (now called dodgeball) though I don't think at that age we really knew what it meant.

The year before Martin Luther King Day became a national holiday, I was in the seventh grade, my first year of junior high. That day, the majority of my classmates protested by refusing to go to class, storming the cafeteria, breaking tables, and causing minor destruction. The local TV station interviewed one of the students and asked, "Why are you guys protesting?" She replied, "Some guy died today." I have long believed that the media selects the most ignorant people for their news clips. I personally did not participate because, like most thirteen-year-olds, I could not see further than a few feet in front of myself and really did not know much about MLK or the movement.

In the 90s, there were two distinct experiences that made a big impression on me. I was working for a short time in a supermarket. The gentleman who I believe was Croatian and spoke little English had the label from a mayonnaise jar and was pointing at it. I escorted him down the proper aisle with shelves stocked full of every type of mayonnaise and found his special brand. That gentleman grabbed hold of me with a large smile, hugged and kissed both checks, and said in broken English, "I love America!"

The second incident was substantially different. I was working at a mini-mart near the Portland airport. A white gentleman with a very southern drawl said, in a conspiratorial tone, "You sure don't have many Black people out here, do you?" I replied we did (keep in mind I had never really been anywhere other than Oregon). He said, "No son. You don't understand." Well, that was true. Something I did not know until many years later was that the Oregon Constitution had language that prohibited Black Americans from living in the state unless they were slaves. I don't know if it's still there, but it was for the twenty-seven years I lived there.

It was not until I came to prison that I started becoming aware of true injustice. There were a few distinct incidents in my first two years. The only prison doctor, who I saw for a migraine headache, directed me to drop my pants for a physical. He conducted the exam by stroking my genitals. I learned that this had happened to several others, so often even the staff talked about it. I and several others filed grievances. Those were not processed, rather they were thrown out and the incidents were suppressed. Ironically, years later the counselor who suppressed the incidents became a sex offender treatment therapist at another prison.

Shortly thereafter, I filed two grievances and a witness statement for a fellow prisoner over legal access and other issues. The immediate response was repetitive infractions (prison rule violations), segregations (the hole), and prison transfers. Since 2005, I have been transferred to seven of this state's prisons and two private prisons out of state and have seen the segregation at each. I have been transferred approximately eleven times with prohibited placement at entire institutions for unspecified safety and security concerns. These generally include segregations around the time of serving or litigating lawsuits against the prison and its staff. This is a very common practice for prisoners who speak out.[1]

A few years ago, I was helping a demographic of the male prison population obtain the right to wear makeup. One of the other factions said, "McKee you're a middle aged pasty white straight guy. Why do you give a shit if they can wear makeup? DOC took our porn away." Do I care one way or the other if someone wears makeup? Not particularly. I do not care about having porn in prison either. What I do care about, and consider my responsibility, is the government oppressing our individual freedoms for no other reason than they can. We are prisoners. Our colors are khaki clothes and ID Green. If I allow the government to oppress one, I will allow them to oppress all.

Back when the slavery of blacks was taking place in the Old South, it was next to a crime for slaves from one plantation to communicate acts of resistance to another plantation. It is against prison rules to correspond with other prisoners, attempt, aid, or organize a group demonstration, work stoppage, or hunger strike. Each facility will reject any

---

1 Kane y. Winn 319 F. Supp. 2d 162, 166-206 (1st Cir. 2004); Silva v. Di Vittorio, 658 F.3d 1090, 1095 (9th Cir. 2010); James E. Robertson "One of the Dirty Secrets of American Corrections Retaliation, Surplus Power, and Whistleblowing Inmates," 42 U. Mich. J.L reform 611 (2009).

communication that suggests such.[2] Although prisoners still pay taxes, they do not have the right to vote in all but two states (Maine/Vermont). The 13th Amendment still requires slavery in the terms of servitude. In theory, our only voice is through the courts but between the retaliatory obstruction of the ability to present claims and the court's unwillingness to intervene, this is a fallacy.[3] Ironically, in late December 2020, the U.S. imposed sanctions on China. Why? Because they suppress "freedom of expression."

The prisons keep us divided and pacified, or more accurately, we allow them. It is a rule violation to gamble or possess gambling paraphernalia.[4] But every institution and unit has a gambling table using state supplied cards. Only when prisoners begin physically fighting over the game does the prison enforce the rule for those specific individuals. They allow a certain amount of drugs and tobacco in. They keep us fighting each other through racial, gang or our crimes. A prisoner once said to me, "Sergeant Richardson's cool. He told me which house was telling on us." The person actually believed the sergeant was doing him a favor. More than likely the person had just pissed off the sergeant, probably by filing a grievance. That sergeant expected the one to fight the other, thereby both going to the hole and leaving the unit.

From the moment I stepped on the chain bus from jail to prison, the guards told us we used to be able to smoke until a prisoner filed a lawsuit. At every orientation at each prison I have been at, there is always at least one staff member that tells us we lost some privilege because some prisoner grieved it. We can get away with a lot in prison, including murder, and the prison will look the other way. But as soon as you start speaking out about the inhumane treatment and violations of the limited rights you have, the full force of prison abuse

---

2 Policy 450 100 Att. 1 #1, 9, 16, 20, 25 27 available at www.doc.wa.gov/policies; Washington Administrative Code (WAC) 137-25-030(1) (650) (651) (652) (682) (746)
3 McKee v. Wash. Dept of Corr,, Division III Court of Appeals No. 378705.Appellants opening Brief should be available by June 30, 2021 at www. Courts.wa.gov
4 WAC 137-25-030(1) (559)

is taken until it either crushes your spirit or convinces those around you to not follow your lead.

What does social justice mean to me? It's a feel-good term for an ugly problem. The same as changing prisoner to incarcerated individual, guard to correctional officer, Warden to Superintendent, and prison to Department of Corrections. It's a feel-good name for the same ugly pig. Freedom is not free. It is a never-ending fight. Until prisoners realize they are slaves of the state, and their power lies in unity through peacefully withholding their slave labor and demanding basic human treatment, social justice is just another fancy name for an unchanged problem.[5]

---

5 "A Call to End Slavery," Summer 2020 Newsletter; "The Dismal State of Affairs of Food Service In Washington Prisons," Winter 2021 Newsletter.

Printed in the USA
CPSIA information can be obtained
at www.ICGtesting.com
CBHW071118050824
12715CB00010B/480